W9-ARZ-788

ERNEST L. BOYER:
SELECTED SPEECHES 1979–1995

Ernest L. Boyer

SELECTED SPEECHES

1979–1995

THE CARNEGIE FOUNDATION
FOR THE ADVANCEMENT OF TEACHING

5 IVY LANE, PRINCETON, NEW JERSEY 08540

This report is published as part of the effort by The Carnegie Foundation for the Advancement of Teaching to explore significant issues in education. The views expressed should not necessarily be ascribed to individual members of the Board of Trustees of The Carnegie Foundation.

Editor: Lauren Maidment Green
Managing Editor: Jan Hempel
Typesetting and Design: Dawn Berberian
Designer: Matthew Young

LIBRARY OF CONGRESS CATALOGING-IN-PUBLICATION DATA

Boyer, Ernest L.
    [Speeches. Selections]
    Ernest L. Boyer, selected speeches, 1979-1995.
       p.   cm.
    Includes bibliographical references (p.).
    ISBN 0-931050-60-X
    1. Education—Aims and objectives—United States. 2. Education,
Higher—United States. 3. Educational change—United States.
I. Title.
LA210.B66 1997
370´.972—dc21   97-24826
                                                   CIP

Copies are available from

JOSSEY-BASS INC., PUBLISHERS
350 Sansome Street, Fifth Floor
San Francisco, California 94104

PHONE (888) 378-2537   FAX (800) 605-2665

Visit our site on the World Wide Web:
http://www.carnegiefoundation.org

Contents

Foreword

THE TENURE OF ERNEST L. BOYER as President of The Carnegie Foundation for the Advancement of Teaching marked one of the most productive and distinguished eras in the Foundation's ninety-year history. His decade and a half of spirited and dedicated leadership yielded a body of work that has informed public policy and helped to shape education reform efforts at all levels.

If one were asked to single out a characteristic that has been constant in all of his work, it would surely be his reverence for language and understanding of the power of words to move minds and forge change. His dedication to civility and clarity in all discourse became a trademark; his ability to speak plainly and eloquently was respected far and wide. Whether serving as Chancellor of the State University of New York in the first half of the 1970s, or as U.S. Commissioner of Education, a post he held prior to joining Carnegie in 1979, Dr. Boyer was first and foremost a communicator—of inspiration, ideas, and challenges to act.

Not surprisingly, this gifted orator was much in demand, and he spoke to countless audiences across America and beyond its shores. He addressed teachers, principals, faculty, and administrators. He also spoke to parents, journalists, artists, corporate leaders, legislators, and students.

Shortly before his death in December 1995, Dr. Boyer, working in consultation with his wife, Kay, developed a list of speeches from his Carnegie years that touched on several of the abiding principles underpinning his work. Many of the speeches chosen for the collection were delivered during the first half of the 1990s, an especially prolific period for Dr. Boyer and the Foundation.

This was the period when he brought many of his ideas full circle, from his seminal work in the 1980s on high school and college, back to the earliest years of life and learning, and to teaching and learning in a new kind of elementary school he called the Basic School. It was during this period, too, that many of the themes of his book *College* were enlarged, most especially a broadened conception of scholarship and the need for engagement beyond the halls of academe.

It is hoped that this collection will provide the reader with a sense of Dr. Boyer's ability to speak powerfully, yet with simplicity. He often spoke extemporaneously and from scribbled notes, revising—always improving— even minutes before a speech was scheduled to begin. Somehow, these efforts consistently emerged as a coherent, compelling whole. Rather than interrupt these remarks with footnotes and citations, a list of references he found particularly inspiring is provided at the end of the collection, along with a complete list of Carnegie publications produced during his tenure.

That Dr. Boyer was able to strike a responsive chord among all of his many and varied listeners stands as an enduring tribute to his life and work. His simple yet profound themes of character, connections, and community still resound today and, one suspects, will do so for many generations to come.

LAUREN MAIDMENT GREEN
former Secretary
The Carnegie Foundation

SCHOOLS

Ready to Learn:
A Mandate for the Nation

33d Charles W. Hunt Memorial Lecture
American Association of Colleges for Teacher Education
San Diego, California
February 17, 1993

I AM DELIGHTED TO JOIN YOU at this 45th annual convention of the American Association of Colleges for Teacher Education. I'm especially pleased to be invited to deliver the Charles W. Hunt lecture, and I extend to everyone assembled in this room my greatest admiration. You are engaged every single day in the heroic task of preparing teachers—professionals who will most profoundly influence future generations—and I know of no other more sacred calling.

This evening I have been asked to talk about the school readiness of children. Perhaps the best place to begin is January 20, 1990, when President George Bush, in his second State of the Union message, announced for the first time in our history six ambitious goals for all of the nation's schools. I found all of the goals fascinating, but I found the first one the most forward looking, the most compelling: that by the year 2000 every child in America will come to school "ready to learn." We understand, of course that children begin to learn even before they take their first breath. With that astonishing notion in mind, we have to realize that what is really being advocated is a national commitment to provide a nourishing climate for very young children so that their first school experiences will be exciting and productive and their potential as students most fully realized.

This is, I understand, an audacious, hugely optimistic proposition. Indeed, some of my friends upon hearing about the first national goal dismissed it as wholly unrealistic. But my response is, "What did you expect the President to say, that by the year 2000, *half* the children will come to school ready to learn?" Dreams can be fulfilled only when they've been defined, and if, during the decade of the 1990s, school readiness would indeed become a mandate for the nation, I am convinced that all of the other goals would in large measure be fulfilled. So let's accept, as an absolutely essential educational and moral obligation, that we will do right by children and pledge that all will come to school well prepared for formal learning.

But how should we proceed? At The Carnegie Foundation last year, we prepared a special report entitled *Ready to Learn: A Mandate for the Nation*. We concluded that if all children are, in fact, to be well prepared for school, seven priorities should be vigorously pursued.

I.

As a first priority for school readiness, every child in this country should have a healthy start, since good health and good education are inextricably interlocked. But we have a very long way to go. The harsh truth is that in America today nearly one-fourth of all children under the age of six is officially classified as poor. One out of five pregnant women in this country has belated prenatal care or none at all. In America today, over forty thousand babies are damaged during pregnancy by the mother's alcohol abuse. More than 10 percent of the children are born to mothers who used cocaine, marijuana, crack, heroin, or amphetamines during pregnancy. And then we wonder why millions of our children come to school each year not well prepared to learn.

During the Foundation's work on this report, over seven thousand kindergarten teachers responded to our survey asking them about the school readiness of children. They reported that the previous year, 35 percent of the children coming into kindergarten were deficient, either linguistically, emotionally, socially, or nutritionally. These children, in fact, had been harmed and were already behind before their first day of school.

It is clear that good nutrition and medical care, prenatally, are consequentially related to school readiness. Health policy and education policy must be linked.

My wife, Kay, is a certified nurse-midwife. She has delivered many babies throughout the years, including seven grandchildren of our own. She has worked with pregnant teenage girls and she has come home night after night talking about children having children. She has described how these teenage girls had, for nine months, nourished their unborn infants on Coke and potato chips. These girls had no knowledge of what was happening to their own bodies even during birth. They were given the basic facts of life in between the labor pains.

In the Carnegie *Ready to Learn* report, we call for full funding of WIC, the federal Women, Infants, and Children nutrition program that gives food to poor mothers and their babies. We also call for a network of primary health clinics in every community in this nation to assure that every mother and every baby is medically well attended. It always strikes me as fascinating that this country has built eighty-three thousand schools from Bangor, Maine, to Honolulu, Hawaii, not as a federal mandate, but as a grassroots commitment to serve the educational needs of our children, but we haven't created a network of neighborhood health clinics to give children access to good health, which is even more important than access to education.

I would hope that, given the interrelationships just discussed, our schools might come to accommodate more of the health services which are so intimately interlocked with educational readiness. Indeed, the linkage seems altogether obvious when "ready to learn" means, above all else, giving every child a healthy start.

II.

The second priority concerns parents. Every child, to be well prepared for school, will need not just a healthy start but also empowered parents. Parents are, after all, the first and most essential teachers. And yet, I'm convinced that the family is a more imperiled institution than the school, and that schools are being asked to do what families and communities and churches have not been able to accomplish.

Several years ago at The Carnegie Foundation, we surveyed five thousand fifth- and eighth-graders, and 40 percent of them said they go home every afternoon to an empty house, and 60 percent said they wished they had more things to do; 60 percent said they wished they could spend more time with their mothers and fathers, and 30 percent said their family never sits down together to eat a meal. While this country is rightly concerned with improving the schools, we also urgently need to focus attention on how to strengthen families, because by the time the child comes to kindergarten, the infrastructure for learning—for better or worse—has already been established.

This foundation that can open the doors for academic excellence simply must be laid in the home. If all children are to be well prepared for school, we must have mothers and fathers who first give love, then language, to their children. Indeed, language begins even before birth as the unborn infant monitors the mother's voice. It's no accident that the three middle ear bones—the hammer, the anvil, and the stirrup—are the only bones that are fully formed at birth. We listen before we speak, and then following birth, language exponentially explodes.

Now that I'm a grandfather and can observe this process unencumbered by burpings and dirty diapers late at night, I'm absolutely dazzled by the capacity of two- and three-year-olds to use language not only for affection but as weapons of assault. When I was growing up in Dayton, Ohio, we used to say, "Sticks and stones may break my bones, but words will never hurt me." What nonsense. Hit me with a stick, but stop the words that penetrate so deeply.

Despite the fact that it happens everywhere constantly, it is remarkable that children learn so quickly how to manage the syntax of this mysterious capacity we call language. I saw in the *Washington Post* several weeks ago a summary of research conducted in Cambridge, England, demonstrating that the phonetic structures of language, the building blocks of language, are established and recognizable by children at eighteen months. Babies are building their framework of language and verbalization in the earliest months. When children come to school, we don't teach them language; we build on a symbol system that is already well established, provided the children grew up in an environment that linguistically empowered them.

Lewis Thomas wrote on one occasion that "childhood is for language." Wouldn't it be wonderful if every home had good books instead of knick-knacks and plastic flowers in the bookshelves? And wouldn't it be great if every child heard good speech and received thoughtful answers to their questions instead of "be quiet" or "go to bed"?

To achieve our educational goals, we propose in the Carnegie report that each state launch a school-based parent education program so that every parent is given opportunities to receive guidance in the essential task of parenting. We urge that all parents read aloud to their children at least thirty minutes every day. And we recommend that every school district organize a preschool PTA to begin building a bridge between the home and the school—not waiting until the child enters kindergarten, but at the time of birth. Historian Will Durant called the family "the nucleus of civilization." For all children to come to school ready to learn, we simply must have empowered parents. Children deserve this security, and parents deserve the privilege.

III.

Beyond a healthy start and empowered parents, school readiness also means quality preschool for every disadvantaged child, to help overcome not just poor nutrition but social and linguistic deprivation, too. I recognize that not all Head Start programs are succeeding, but the evidence is overwhelming that a quality preschool experience, especially for children most at risk, can be enormously beneficial. And yet millions of needy children are neglected.

Frankly, I consider it a national disgrace that nearly thirty years after Head Start was authorized by Congress, less than 40 percent of the eligible children are being served. What's the analogy? It's like having a vaccine for a dread disease and callously and capriciously denying it to children. How is it that America can spend $100 billion to bail out the savings and loans? How is it that we can spend $300 billion each year on national defense? How is it that we can continue to send space shuttles into orbit and never seem to have enough money for our children?

Well, the good news is that President Clinton has declared his commitment to fully fund Head Start. Let's get that established. But our next goal must be to raise the salaries of preschool teachers and bring more dignity and more status to these unsung heroes. It's just amazing to me how much we neglect those who are teaching the children at the very time children are learning the most. These teachers do the most and, frankly, get the least. It provides a sobering commentary on providing funding of children's needs.

IV.

Fourth, to achieve school readiness we simply must have family-friendly policies in the workplace, so that working parents can spend more time with their children. I'm often invited by corporate leaders to come and speak with them about what they can do to help education. Should they adopt a school? Or should they send them hardware? And I end up saying, "What you should do is remind yourselves that you're employing the parents of school children. It's your obligation to develop policies that allow parents to be available, not just in the workplace, but for parent functions, too."

In yesterday's agrarian society most families lived on farms, and mothers and fathers and their children worked side by side. I grew up helping in a family business. We struggled during the Depression, and when I went home at night, I worked with my father and my mother and with my brothers. I knew if there was no work, there was no bread. Life for most people during those years was hard, the hours were long, but work life and family life were inextricably intertwined.

Today all of that has changed. Most parents work outside the home, including 60 percent of all mothers with preschool children. And according to the distinguished sociologist at Berkeley, Arlie Hochschild, "The job culture has expanded at the expense of the family culture."

In the new Carnegie report, we insist that school readiness must involve the workplace. We call for flex-time arrangements so that work and family obligations can be better blended. We call for more child care programs in the workplace. We propose parenting days. Why not periodically give parents time off with pay, so mothers and fathers can spend time with their children in day care centers and in preschools?

And I would like to see the first day of school in this country become a time of national celebration, an occasion for which every working parent sending a child to school for the first time would have a full day off, with pay, to spend at the school. Instead of just dropping the child off, the parent could help further establish the essential partnership between the school and the family.

Above all, we propose in our report a national parent leave program so that parents can bond with newborns. Kay has convinced me that the first minutes, hours, and weeks of life between the parents and the child are crucial. Human bonding is essential. Touching and holding matter very much in the emotional development of children. Yet, somehow we have not allowed that essential reality in human life experience to be reaffirmed in the workplace policies in this country.

In Finland, working women get thirty-five weeks of parental leave with full salary. In Japan, women have the right to a three-month leave at 60 percent pay. In Germany, mothers are eligible for a fully paid leave beginning six weeks before birth and ending six weeks after. I found it disturbing that, on two separate occasions, a modest family leave bill, which would have allowed leave without pay, was vetoed by the President. I celebrate the fact that the bill was one of the first legislative actions by the new Congress and has now been ratified into law.

Sociologist Robert Bellah said, "It might appear at the moment, when economic competitiveness is such an obsession, that Americans 'can't afford' to think about the family. . . . Nothing," he said, "could be more shortsighted. In the long run our economic life . . . depends on the quality of people." I would add, that it depends on the quality of our families, too, who are deeply affected by public policies.

Thus far, I have focused on four priorities for school readiness that touch directly on the family: a healthy start, empowered parents, quality preschool, and family-friendly policies in the workplace. However, beyond these four inner rings, there are three "outer rings" in the larger social context that also shape the lives of children.

V.

Surely the most powerful and most pervasive influence in a child's life, beyond the parent, is TV, which penetrates almost every home and profoundly shapes the environment of our children. The harsh truth is that America's 19 million preschoolers watch television 14 billion hours—I repeat, 14 billion hours—every single year. They are glued to the screen two to three hours every single day. And, yet, what they see is enormously depressing.

On Saturday morning during the so-called "children's hour," the youngsters of this country are served up a steady diet of junk food commercials and cartoons that contain, on average, twenty-six acts of violence every single hour. And then we wonder why we have troubled children, failing schools, and violence on the streets. Frankly, I consider it a shocking indictment of our culture that not one of the four major television networks—ABC, CBS, NBC, or FOX—has a single hour of educational programming devoted exclusively to young children.

In response to this neglect, we propose in the Carnegie report that a Ready-to-Learn children's channel be created. After all, we have channels for news, and channels for sports, and channels for weather, and channels for sex, and channels for selling junk jewelry. Is it unthinkable that we would have at least one channel devoted exclusively to the well-being of our children?

There is some good news here. Congress, just last fall, passed what was labeled a "Ready-to-Learn" bill, sponsored successfully by Senator Edward Kennedy, that establishes a preschool programming authorization for PBS stations all across the country.

And just two months ago I received a letter from the president of the Learning Channel telling me that after our report was received and read, his board of directors met and determined that the Learning Channel would devote six hours of noncommercial programming for preschool children every single day. I'm happy to report that the series, called *Ready, Set, Learn*, which runs from 6:00 a.m. to noon, is already on the air. This is clearly public service programming at its very best. It gives us hope.

In the summer of 1938, essayist E. B. White said, "I believe television is going to be the test of the modern world. . . . We shall discover either a new and unbearable disturbance of the general peace or a saving radiance in the sky. We shall stand or fall by television," White said, "of that I am quite sure." It seems to me that that challenge is even more urgent now. And I am convinced that if the nation's 19 million preschoolers are to be well prepared, we simply must have television that enriches rather than degrades.

VI.

Beyond television, which impacts the child's life and penetrates the home, children are also influenced by the neighborhoods that surround them—by the environment they encounter on the street. There was a time when neighborhoods were safe, supportive places for children. I remember playing on the street—kick-the-can, red light/green light, and hide-and-seek—and somehow there were always little nooks and crannies for children to crawl in and no one worried very much.

In recent years we have built cities that are more concerned about cars than kids. During the past fifty years, in the name of urban renewal, we have constructed glitzy banks and glittering new hotels that look like Taj Mahals. We have erected high-rise apartments and office towers that soar into the sky. We have built dazzling shopping centers and high-speed highways, but somehow we have forgotten about the children. For them there is no place to go, no place safe.

Several years ago at The Carnegie Foundation, in response to our survey of fifth- and eighth-graders, more than half of these students agreed that, "there are not a lot of good places to play in my neighborhood." One eighth-grader spoke for many when she said, "I'm afraid. I'm often scared to go back and forth to school." And in the most improbable place of Madison, Wisconsin, a teacher told a Carnegie researcher, "Many of my children come to school worrying about the violence they may encounter in the neighborhood."

In response to this scandalous neglect, we recommend in the Carnegie report that every city, town, and village recommit itself to building a network of outdoor, and even indoor parks. While many cities have used up virtually every inch of ground, they still have lots of unused interior spaces which could be converted into interior parks for children. Also, let's occasionally close off some city streets to create instant playgrounds for our children. How many streets do we need to build that continue to be congested and polluted while our children increasingly are crowded off the streets and off the sidewalks? They need places to gather and places to play.

In the Carnegie report, we also propose that all libraries and museums and zoos be well funded and establish school readiness programs for preschoolers. And we urge that every shopping mall have a ready-to-learn center built in, a place where young children could engage in play and learning. After all, the shopping mall has replaced the early village green. It's where the children go. It's where the teenagers go. It's where families gather.

Further, I'm convinced the time has come to consider enhancing the school board with a children's board, to shift the focus from the bureaucracy of education to the needs of children. Let's begin to integrate services within the schools and create, around every school, neighborhoods for learning.

VII.

Finally, school readiness will succeed only as we begin to build connections across the generations. Margaret Mead wrote on one occasion that the health of any culture is sustained by at least three generations vitally interacting with one another. This important connection is our seventh priority.

Looking back, the most important mentor in my own life was my Grandfather Boyer, who incidentally lived to be one hundred years old. When he was about ninety-six, I asked Grandfather about the schooling that he had had. "Well," he said, "I went to school about six years, but I went only in the winter when I wasn't needed on the farm," which tells you about school and family life in the 1880s. When Grandpa was forty, he moved his little family into the slums of Dayton, Ohio. He spent the next forty years running a city mission, working for the poor, meeting the needs of those who had been pathetically neglected, teaching them. He taught me, as I observed his life, that to be truly human one must serve.

I remember Grandma Boyer, who was at full height 4 foot 8, standing on the porch of the mission and holding little sack lunches. And four or five big, hulky men would come down from the railroad tracks, "hobos," as we used to call them, standing in front of her with their heads bowed, and holding hat in hand, while she said a prayer on their behalf before she passed out the lunches. These memories are so vivid they will stay with me to my dying day. Yet, for far too many children the intergenerational models have dramatically and tragically diminished.

In America today, we're creating a "horizontal culture," one in which each generation is isolated from the others. We are organizing ourselves by layers. Infants are in nurseries, toddlers are in day care, older children are organized by age levels in the schools—fifth, sixth, seventh—college students go off to college campuses, and adults increasingly spend their time in the workplace or commuting back and forth. And older citizens increasingly are retreating into retirement villages or restricted neighborhoods with covenants in which children are just not welcome. They, too, are living and dying all alone. I find something strange and unhealthy about a retirement village where the average age is eighty and, just as unhealthy, a day care center where the average age is four, where children speak mostly to their peers. This segregation does not need to be tolerated and shouldn't be.

But as I look ahead, I see an alarming possibility that we will increasingly have something akin to demographic warfare in public policy: a struggle for money that pits older people against the young. In the battle that has gone on for about a decade, older people are winning and poor children are losing because children remain voiceless in the struggle.

Clearly, the time has come to break up the age ghettos and build intergenerational institutions that bring the old and the young together. For several years my own parents lived in a retirement village where the average age was eighty. My father said, "No big deal being eighty around this place. You have to be ninety just to get a cake." The good news is they had a day care center there and every morning about fifty three- and four-year-olds came trucking in. Every little day care center enrollee had an adopted grandparent, so when I called my father, he wouldn't talk about his aches and pains; he would talk about his little friend who he was sure was going to be governor and perhaps President some day. And when I would visit him, just like any proud grandparent, he would have the child's artwork taped on the wall and proudly describe the productions of last week.

There is something magical about bringing the old and young together. That's the way life was intended. We're losing something in a culture in which there is a disconnectedness, in which the continuity of living is not somehow conveyed in a normal and natural way. Through intergenerational connections, children can see the courage and the agony of growing older and older people can be inspired by the energy and innocence of youth. If school readiness is our goal, we simply must find ways to strengthen connections across the generations so young people can gain perspective, as well as feel cared for. This contact can only provide benefits for all.

In summary, school readiness means a healthy start, quality preschool, empowered parents, a responsive workplace, television that teaches, neighborhoods for learning, and connections across the generations. To put it simply, school readiness means creating in this country a public love of children.

But here I should make an absolutely crucial point. While all children must be well prepared for school, it's equally important that all schools be ready for the children. At The Carnegie Foundation, as a follow-up to the ready-to-learn report, we're now completing a sequel that we have tentatively entitled *The Basic School*, which calls for restructuring primary education.

The Basic School would combine kindergarten through grade five. It would engage all parents in what we're calling "a covenant for learning." It would include integrated services. It would include cooperative learning. And in the Basic School, there would be no class with more than fifteen students.

Frankly, I find it ludicrous when people say—and I have actually heard a Secretary of Education say—that class size doesn't matter. I don't think he's been in a classroom in forty years. To say it doesn't matter, especially in the early years which is precisely the time when children need one-on-one attention, is not only an insult to children, but an embarrassment to common sense. I've never taught kindergarten or first grade, though I did teach deaf children in one-on-one situations. But I do have grandchildren, and frankly, just taking four or five of them to McDonald's is a hugely complicated task. I come home a basket case. Getting on the boots, and taking all the orders, which change every ten seconds, and wiping up the milkshake, and keeping ketchup and mustard off the floor, I mean, these are logistical problems of great magnitude. Now, translate that to the classroom—and many of you have been there. Teachers have to do all these kinds of things, and at the same time they are expected to move the minds and hearts of these children along individually and empower them for learning. I'm convinced that most school critics couldn't survive one week in the classrooms they so vigorously condemn.

In the Basic School report, in addition to suggesting a revised structure for the school, we're proposing a new, integrated curriculum based not on the old Carnegie units but on what we call the eight commonalities that bind us all together. We also insist in our report that there should be no national standardized testing of children during the first four years of formal education.

More than thirty years ago, Kay and I were called into the school by officials who reported with some anxiousness that one of our children had been declared a "special student," and you know what that means. He was described as a "special student" because of his performance, we learned, on a single test and because, as another teacher put it, "He's a dreamer." Well, our son did dream, of course. He dreamed about the stars and about places far away. And he dreamed about how he could get out of school, but we were absolutely convinced that he was gifted and that somehow his talents just didn't match the routine of the classroom or the rigidity of the test.

Well, let the record show that for ten years this so-called "special student" has lived successfully in a Mayan village. He knows the language. He understands the culture. He runs Mayan schools. He builds fantastic bridges. He has a wonderful family, with four children. He has survived living under conditions that might have totally defeated not only his father but the psychometricians who concluded years ago that he couldn't learn.

Recently, I reflected on why the testers were so wrong, and suddenly it occurred to me that the answer was quite simple: the problem was, they didn't have a test on how to survive in a Mayan village. They didn't have a test on how to build a bridge. They didn't have an examination on how to understand the beauty of another culture.

James Agee wrote on one occasion that "with every child who is born, under no matter what circumstances, the potentiality of the human race is born again." And what we urgently need today, in my opinion, is to declare a moratorium on all of this testing mania and devote our energies to the careful development of new assessment procedures that would focus not just on verbal intelligence but on social intelligence and intuitive intelligence, aesthetic and spatial intelligence. We need tests that measure something more than that which matters least. And meanwhile we must encourage the potentials in children to flourish.

Let me add finally that if all schools are to be ready for children, we simply must give more dignity and more status to teachers, especially in the early grades. In the end, excellence in education means excellence in teaching, and if this country would give the status to first grade teachers that we give to full professors, this one act alone would revitalize the nation's schools.

I respectfully suggest to President Clinton that he invite the Teachers of the Year from all fifty states to a formal dinner in the East Room of the White House, and this should be televised prime time. After all, we invite visiting dignitaries from overseas, why not invite the dignitaries from the classrooms in the United States who are themselves the heroes of the nation?

To emphasize the point once more: The nation's first education goal, readiness for all, is in my judgment the most important domestic challenge for this country. It is not just Washington's business, it's everybody's business. It's a pledge that America has made not only to itself but most especially to its children. And I can only ask you, what is crueler than making a pledge to children and then walking away? Are we serious about readiness to learn? This isn't just a campaign slogan; this is a moral obligation we have made to the coming generation. And while preparing all children for school, let's also prepare all schools for children, giving top priority in this country to the first ten years of life.

Recently, my good friend Marian Wright Edelman sent me a copy of a prayer, and it occurred to me that, with a bit of paraphrasing, this prayer might be an appropriate way to close my remarks tonight. The prayer reads,

> Dear Lord, we pray for children who like to be tickled, who sneak popsicles before dinner, and who can never find their shoes. And we also pray for children who can't run down the street in a new pair of sneakers, who never get dessert, who don't have any rooms to clean

up, and whose pictures aren't on anybody's dresser. Dear Lord, we pray for children who spend all their allowances before Tuesday, who throw tantrums in the grocery store, who pick at their food, who squirm in church and in the temple, who scream into the phone. And we also pray for children whose nightmares come in the light of day, who rarely see a doctor, who have never seen a dentist, who aren't spoiled by anybody, and who go to bed hungry and cry themselves to sleep. We pray for those we smother with love, and we pray especially for those who will grab the hand of anybody kind enough to hold it.

Children are our most precious resource. In the end, they're all we have. And if we as a nation cannot help the coming generation, if we cannot prepare all children for learning and for life, then just what will bring America together?

The Basic School

National Association of Elementary School Principals
San Diego, California
April 11, 1995

THIS YEAR THE CARNEGIE FOUNDATION released a major new report called *The Basic School: A Community for Learning*, which focuses on elementary education. While preparing this report, researchers at the Foundation visited literally dozens of elementary schools from coast to coast. We were in hundreds of classrooms, and I was profoundly impressed, time and time again, by the eagerness of students, by the dedication of teachers, and by the commitment of the principals. Teachers and principals are performing heroic acts every single day, succeeding often under enormously difficult conditions. By the conclusion of our study I became convinced that most school critics could not survive one week in the schools and the classrooms they so vigorously condemn.

I also concluded that the last thing we need in American education is another report that goes on the shelf. The last thing we need is another "pilot project." The last thing we need is another innovation that promises excellence by the year 2000. What we really need is to take the school reform movement back to the beginning, to the first years of formal learning, to the elementary school, which is by any measure transcendently the most important. We need to go into every classroom, where teachers meet with students, because that's where excellence in education begins and ends. Above all, it's time to stop looking for quick fixes and promising panaceas and begin to put into place the tried-and-true practices that really work.

After reading the literature, consulting with experts, and surveying thousands of principals, teachers, students, and parents in twelve countries around the world, we concluded that there are, in fact, four priorities—as simple as that sounds—four qualities of elementary education that are the essential building blocks to achieve excellence for all.

COMMUNITY

We say in the new Carnegie report that building a true community of learning is the first and most essential ingredient of an effective school. We found, in our study, that it is simply impossible to achieve educational excellence at a school where purposes are blurred, where teachers and students fail to communicate thoughtfully with each other, and where parents are uninvolved in the education of their children. Community is, without question, the glue that holds an effective school together, as Principal Alicia Thomas at Jackson-Keller School in San Antonio, Texas, told us.

But community doesn't just happen. By community, we mean something far more than a sentimental slogan or a message to be sent home to parents at the beginning of the year. What we really are talking about is the culture of the school, the way people relate to one another, their attitudes and values. We concluded that to achieve community, a school must have six essential qualities. The school must be a *purposeful* place, with a clear and vital mission. The school must be a *communicative* place, where people speak and listen with care to each other. The school must be a *just* place, where everyone is treated fairly. The school must be a *disciplined* place, where clearly defined rules of conduct are established. The school must be a *caring* place, where students feel secure. And, finally, the school, to be a community, must be a *celebrative* place, with ceremonies and other times when everyone in the school comes together.

And to create this spirit of community we conclude that the Basic School also should be small enough to assure that every student will be known by name. During my days as Commissioner I would often visit large, overcrowded schools, where only the good and bad students were known. And I'd conclude that many students dropped out simply because no one noticed that they had, in fact, "dropped in."

For the community we envision to come alive, teachers must have time to work together, ideally, once a week, with the principal as lead teacher, who guides the institution more by inspiration than by directive. Lillian Brinkley, principal at the Willard Model School in Norfolk, Virginia, captured the spirit of the principal's role when she said, "I believe that leadership is the ability to inspire others. I don't ask teachers to do anything I wouldn't do."

I found it enormously significant in our national survey that nearly 70 percent of the elementary school teachers in this country rate the performance of the principal of their school "excellent" or "good." I want to congratulate all of them not only for staying in the trenches, responding to the questions of the community, getting caught in the crossfire of ideological debates, but also for being able to give a steady hand and inspiration to the teachers who meet with children every single day. That's a great accomplishment for which they should be appreciated, not criticized, by the public.

I'm suggesting then, that a school community begins with teachers, and with the principal acting as lead teacher. But, in the Basic School, the circle of community quickly extends outward to include the parents, who are, after all, the child's first and most essential teachers. We hear a lot of talk these days about how the schools have failed, and, certainly, education can improve. And yet, as time passes, the more I'm becoming convinced it's not the school that has failed, it's the partnership that's failed. Today, schools are being asked to do what homes and communities and religious institutions have not been able to accomplish. And if they fail anywhere along the line, we condemn them for not meeting our high-minded expectations. Thirty years of research reveal that it's simply impossible to have an island of educational excellence in a sea of community indifference. If we hope to achieve quality in the nation's schools, parents simply must become actively involved, not in running schools, but in helping in the education of their own children.

Sam Sava, the distinguished leader of the National Association of Elementary School Principals, said it best when he said that children absorb as many unspoken lessons about love and work in their homes as they do the spoken lessons of the classroom. And Secretary of Education Richard Riley echoed this same conviction when he said, "The American family is the rock on which a solid education can and must be built."

Simply put, in the Basic School, building community is the first and most essential goal, with teachers and the principal and parents engaged in common cause on behalf of children.

CURRICULUM

Beyond building community, the second building block of the Basic School is a curriculum with coherence, which begins with proficiency in language. Language is, without question, central to all learning. Our sophisticated use of symbols distinguishes us from all other forms of life, the porpoise and the bumblebee notwithstanding, and connects us to each other.

Consider the miracle of this very moment. I stand here vibrating my vocal folds, and molecules go scurrying in your direction, they hit your tympanic membrane, and symbols go up your eighth cranial nerve, and there's a response deep in your cerebrum that, I trust, approximates the images in mine. But do you realize the audacity of this very act? This assumption that somehow we're intellectually and evocatively connected?

Children encounter language even before birth, as the unborn infant monitors the mother's voice, and then following birth, language exponentially explodes. By the time a child marches off to school, she or he knows at least three thousand words and is able to use them in powerfully penetrating ways.

So the task of the elementary school is not to teach children language. The task is to build on the symbol system that's God-given and already well in place. Lewis Thomas, the great essayist, captured the spirit of the Basic School when he said that childhood is for language. And in the Basic School, every student is expected to read with comprehension, write with clarity, and effectively speak and listen. But I should hurriedly add that, in the Basic School, language is defined broadly to include not just words, but mathematics, as well as the universal symbol system of the arts.

The arts are not a "frill" in the Basic School. The arts speak a majestic language that words cannot convey, and, once again, young children know this language very well. They respond to rhythm, to music, to dance, and to color, even before they can articulate words. For several years, I taught children who were deaf. I was always struck by the frustration of a child unable to reach out with words and speak and listen to others. Some of the children would lash out and hit others. But the same children engaged in the arts were an altogether different sight. When they put paint on paper, or followed the rhythm of music through the vibrations of their fingers, or began to weave, or worked with clay, you could see a transformation as they began to express visually the feelings and emotions deep inside them. They were using the arts as a language, as a symbol system, to convey what they could not express with words, and the arts became the symbol system of preference for these children.

Several years ago, when the world-renowned physicist Victor Weisskopf was asked, "What gives you hope in troubled times?" he replied, "Mozart and quantum mechanics." I was intrigued the other day when I read an interview with the latest Westinghouse Science Talent Search winner, a fifteen-year-old boy by the name of Aleksandr Khazanov. Asked why he stays awake late at night doing mathematics equations, Khazanov didn't say, "Well, I'm intellectually engaged with the formulas." He said that mathematics makes beautiful ideas, beautiful proofs. For him, there was beauty in the symbol system of mathematics.

Where do words and numbers and the arts begin and end? It's a symbol system that's coherent. Mathematics is beautiful. Equations can be aesthetically pleasing. In the Basic School all students become proficient not only in the symbol system we call words, but also in numbers and in the arts.

Beyond proficiency in language, all students in the Basic School study a solid general education curriculum with coherence. During our study, we found that often the elementary school curriculum is disturbingly disconnected. Teachers make countless lesson plans, but often with no pattern or broader design that would give students a greater perspective. Children complete the isolated units, they move relentlessly from one grade level to the next, but what they fail to gain is a more coherent view of knowledge and a more integrated, more authentic view of life.

We observed that children come to school in kindergarten filled with curiosity. They're endlessly asking questions. They keep asking *"Why?"* But somewhere around grade four they stop asking *why*, and begin to ask, "Will we have this on the test?" And those two questions tell more about the nature of the inquiry than any other observation to be made. *"Why?"* is a curiosity question. "Will we have this on the test?" is a conformity question, conformity to the system. Mortimer Adler asked on one occasion, "What happens between the nursery and college to turn the flow of questions off?" One thing that happens is a curriculum in which students study the pieces but never see the patterns. We're gearing them up for the SATs and for the academic disciplines that faculties have imposed on kindergarten, when we should be integrating in the college what kindergartners are always asking.

We propose, then, in the Basic School, a new curriculum, one that is coherent. Specifically, we suggest that all of the traditional academic subjects—from science, to history, to civics, to literature—might all be fitted within eight integrative themes that we believe cover the territory of knowledge, but provide integration, too. And these eight integrative themes are based on the universal human experiences we all share. Is it possible that all people have eight common experiences? While we recognize human diversity, I think we must urgently start teaching students about human community as well.

In the Basic School we suggest that these eight themes, which we call "core commonalities," include: the Life Cycle, the Use of Symbols, Membership in Groups, a Sense of Time and Space, a Response to the Aesthetic, Producing and Consuming, Connections to Nature, and Living with Purpose. Every subject could find a home within these themes, so that knowledge would relate not so much to the academic disciplines as to students' lives. At The Carnegie Foundation, we are developing a curriculum framework within each of these eight commonalities, as well as sample lesson plans, which might be used by schools. Also, teachers in schools across the country are working on new curriculum materials and lesson plans using the commonalities, which spiral upward through grade five or six.

The Milford School District in Delaware recently announced that it was going to introduce the human commonalities curriculum from kindergarten through grade twelve. And Kae Keister, who is the principal at the Banneker School in Delaware, is working, along with her teachers, on units of study for the core commonalities, as are other principals across the country. Summer institutes are also being planned. Principals and superintendents are saying that this curriculum will not only help students discover the disciplines, but it will help the schools meet state standards, too.

Simply stated, the thematic approach to the curriculum, which spirals upward vertically, not only gives students a core of essential knowledge, it also helps them discover connections across the disciplines and helps them understand, as well, how what they learn in the classroom relates to life.

More than fifty years ago, Mark Van Doren wrote, "The connectedness of things is what the educator contemplates to the limit of his capacity." He concluded by saying, "The student who can begin early in life to see things as connected has begun the life of learning." And I'm suggesting that discovering the connections is what the Basic School is all about.

Before leaving the curriculum, I should stress the point that the Basic School is committed to assessment. High academic standards, achievement standards, and benchmarks will be set, for both literacy and general knowledge. And in the Basic School, the goal of assessment is to affirm and expand the potential of every child, not to restrict it.

CLIMATE

Beyond building community, and beyond offering a curriculum with coherence, an effective school provides a climate for learning that is both active and creative, not passive and restrictive. Several years ago, I walked unannounced into a fifth-grade classroom in New Haven. I observed thirty children crowded around the teacher's desk, and my first impulse was to hurry down the hall and report the crisis to the central office. But I paused and discovered that what I was observing was not a crisis, it was a magic moment. The children had just finished reading Charles Dickens' *Oliver Twist*, and they were debating vigorously whether little Oliver could make it in their own home town. And they concluded that while he was able to survive in far-off London, he never would have made it in New Haven, a much tougher city. They had discovered how great literature relates to the reality of life.

The simple truth is that excellence in education is that magic moment between curious students and an inspired teacher. But for teachers to succeed, we need smaller classes, especially in the primary grades, where young children often need one-on-one attention.

I have been startled by people who say that class size doesn't matter. Indeed, some people in high positions in education have reached that conclusion. I have to think that they have not spent five minutes with more than three children in the last thirty years. And yet our data show that on average, the elementary school classrooms across the country enroll twenty-six. When we surveyed kindergarten teachers several years ago, we found that in one state the average kindergarten class size is forty-one. And then we have the audacity to talk about being world-class in math and science.

The Basic School would have, as well, flexible class scheduling throughout the day, so that the clock would be adjusted to the lessons, and not the other way around. We also recommend that students be grouped in a variety of ways. We reject the old graded versus nongraded debate. That's an either-or approach that doesn't work. We suggest at least five different grouping patterns in the school, and the children would move flexibly from one to the other, through the day and the week. We suggest homeroom grouping, for a sense of family; mixed-age grouping, for cooperative learning; focused grouping, for concentrated study and coaching; individual grouping, for independent study; and all-school grouping, for community building. The point is that in the Basic School, the grouping pattern fits the purpose.

And we also recommend, in the Basic School, grouping across the generations. Children learn from older people, and we must recognize the need within our isolated institutions for intergenerational connections.

Several years ago it occurred to me that one of the most important people in my own life was my Grandfather Boyer, who lived to be one hundred. At the age of forty, Grandpa Boyer moved his little family from a pleasant residential neighborhood in Dayton, Ohio, into the slum area, as it was called in those days. He lived in that community for forty years, running a city mission to help the poor. There were no social agencies in those days. As I watched my grandfather work with people who were impoverished, I began to understand that to be truly human, one must serve. And I learned from him, not so much from the words he spoke as from the deeds he performed, lessons I could not have learned in school. We cannot deny our children the lessons of intergenerational connections.

Margaret Mead said that the strength of a culture is sustained as three generations vitally interact. And yet I think it's not unfair to say we're building in this country a kind of horizontal culture, in which each age group is separated from the others. Infants are in nurseries, and toddlers in day care. Children in school are organized consistently by age. Young people go off to college and spend four years isolated on campus. Older adults are spending more and more time in the workplace, away from their families for up to ten hours every day, according to recent research. And elder people are living all alone, in retirement villages.

My own parents chose to live in a retirement village for several years, but their village had a day care center, and every day about forty three- and four-year olds would come in. Each child had an adopted grandparent, and intergenerational connections were made every day. When you see this connection, you realize that young people need to observe the difficulty and courage of growing older, and older people need the inspiration of the very young. These are lessons that cannot be taught in an isolated school.

We recommend, in the Basic School, that there be grandteacher programs in the school, and other ways of bringing the old and young together. We must find, in this country, a way to resolve the emerging political conflict between children and older people. We must find institutional arrangements that build bridges across the generations. At the David Cox Elementary School in Charlotte, North Carolina, for example, the children have developed a relationship with the retired people in the village just down the road. The Basic School, then, helps to build connections between the generations.

The climate of the Basic School also is established, of course, with basic resources, from building blocks to books, and includes, as well, the new technology that can connect children in classrooms to networks of knowledge all around the world. And we also urge that every Basic School have health and counseling services for children who are in need.

One of the saddest parts of our study was the frequency with which principals and teachers told us about children who are neglected and abused. One Friday afternoon, we talked to a group of tired teachers at an elementary school in a Midwest city, and the conversation turned immediately to troubled children. One veteran fourth-grade teacher said, "I've taught for many years, and I've never seen children hurting as frequently as they are today." And then she added, rather poignantly, "I know that I'm supposed to teach the basics, but how can I neglect these children who are troubled and abused?"

Several years ago at The Carnegie Foundation we surveyed five thousand fifth- and eighth-graders, and 36 percent said they go home every afternoon to an empty house. Sixty percent said they wished they could spend more time with their mothers and fathers. Two thirds said they wished they had more things to do. And 30 percent said that their family never sits down together to eat a meal.

I believe that America is losing sight of its children. In decisions made every day, we are putting them at the very bottom of the agenda. And while people endlessly criticize the schools, I've concluded that the school is probably the *least* imperiled institution in our culture. The family is a more imperiled institution. The health care system is in deeper trouble than the school. The judicial system is in greater crisis than the school, and I am still wondering what SAT score we should give to Congress.

What I'm suggesting is that we are focusing on the wrong issue. The schools are becoming the solution to everyone else's problem. In many neighborhoods, the school is, in fact, the only institution that is still working. I have gone into neighborhoods where it looked like a bombed-out area. The branch library had closed and was boarded up. There wasn't a health care clinic within five miles. Churches had moved to the suburbs. And guess what? Good old P.S. 104 was still open every single day. And then we have the gall to say that it's the school that's failed.

We struggled, in our report, with these issues. I do not think that schools can solve every social and economic problem. On the other hand, they cannot ignore children who are hungry, neglected, and abused. We sought to find, in the Basic School report, a middle ground. We propose that every school should have at least a health and counseling professional to handle the basic physical and emotional needs of children. But we strongly urge that the school take the lead in trying to build a partnership with other social agencies in the neighborhood, to deal with problems that are more acute and to help rebuild the sense of community, not just within the school, but within the neighborhood as well. All to save the children.

Children are, after all, our most precious resource. And if we as a nation cannot commit ourselves to help the coming generation, if local communities cannot work collectively on behalf of children, then I do wonder what will bring this country back together. And I must confess that as we were completing our study, one of the deepest convictions that I had was that it's time to try to rebuild in this country what I call a "public love of children."

CHARACTER

Thus far, I have considered three of the four priorities for the Basic School: bringing people together to build community, bringing the curriculum together to achieve coherence, and bringing resources together to enrich learning. The fourth building block of the Basic School we call, "A Commitment to Character." It relates the lessons of the classroom to the ethical and moral lives of students. Will everything we propose for the Basic School achieve change for children that will help them learn to live ethical, upright lives?

There was a time when the focus of public education was on the whole child: body, mind, and spirit. Values taught at home were reinforced at school. In 1837, Horace Mann, the father of the common school, insisted that public schools should help students develop *reason* and *conscience*. And the highest and noblest goal of education, Mann said, pertains to our moral character. Schools, he said, should teach virtue before knowledge.

Today, not only has this commitment to teach values before knowledge dramatically declined, but we now feel uncomfortable even talking about such matters. It's all right these days to talk about high academic standards, but it's not all right to talk about ethical standards.

I believe that knowledge unguided by an ethical and moral compass is more dangerous than ignorance itself. The British philosopher George Steiner described the challenge. He said, "We know now that a man can read Goethe or Rilke in the evening, that he can play Bach and Schubert, and go to his day's work at Auschwitz in the morning." And then Steiner asked a fundamental question educators eventually must ask: "What grows up inside literate civilization that seems to prepare it for barbarism?" What grows up, of course, is information without knowledge, knowledge without wisdom, competence without conscience.

The harsh truth is that America's children are growing up in a world that glorifies violence and sexual degradation. They are bombarded with examples of evil actions. And the so-called "children's time" on Saturday morning TV brings our children twenty-six acts of violence every single hour. And then some people have the audacity to suggest that the nation's *schools* are undermining the morals of our children.

The poet Vachel Lindsay wrote: "It is the world's one crime its babes grow dull, ... / Not that they sow, but that they seldom reap, / Not that they serve, but have no gods to serve, / Not that they die but that they die like sheep." We see so many children today unguided and uninspired, even put down, before they have discovered who they are, or fully understand what they might become. The tragedy then is not death. Children must discover that the tragedy is to die with commitments undefined, with convictions undeclared, and with service unfulfilled.

So, the fourth priority of the Basic School is, unapologetically, a commitment to character. And we propose seven core virtues which we believe are appropriate for every school and for every student. Specifically, we suggest that every elementary school commit itself to teach, by word and deed, such old-fashioned virtues as integrity, respect for others, responsibility, compassion, self-discipline, perseverance, and giving to others through an act of service. And these virtues are not just intended for our children. They are intended for ourselves. These are virtues which represent the essence of an educated person. Our work is to come together to model these for children. We must not send conflicting signals to our children, telling them how to behave while we ourselves violate the code of conduct of a civilized society.

Ultimately, children need to learn that to be truly human, one must serve others. Martin Luther King, Jr., said, ". . .[E]verybody can be great because everybody can serve." And I do believe the children of this country are ready to be inspired by a larger vision. Shortly before his death, a Jewish leader, Abraham Joshua Heschel, was asked what message he had for young people and he replied, "Let them remember that there is a meaning beyond absurdity. Let them be sure that every little deed counts, that every word has power, and that we can—everyone—do our share to redeem the world in spite of all absurdities and all frustrations and all disappointments." "And above all," he said, "let them remember that the meaning of life is to build a life as if it were a work of art."

In the end, the Basic School is committed to building lives as if they were works of art. And this is accomplished as the Basic School becomes a community with a clear and vital mission; as it has a curriculum with coherence; as it has a climate for creative learning; as it makes a commitment, ultimately, to build character, not just within children, but within the community as well.

Let me underscore one absolutely essential point. Every single proposal that we make in the Basic School is going on somewhere in schools across this country. This is not a top-down report. It's a bubble-up report. It's an attempt to summarize the best practices that we saw in schools all across this country. What we're proposing is that the best practices all be brought together in what we've called the Basic School, which is not a new institution, but an idea. With this idea we affirm the essentials of effective education while keeping the belief that every single school should still follow its own way and should develop its own distinctive mission.

We are now creating in Princeton an arrangement for developing what might be called a national conversation about the Basic School. We've already set up a special telephone line at the Foundation, and working with Sam Sava and NAESP, we have developed a Basic School computer connection to America On-Line. I've invited every principal who would be inclined to join us in this informal Basic School Network to exchange ideas and information. The goal is not to achieve uniformity, but to stir creativity through the brilliant examples that are already established in schools all across the country. Our goal is to support the nation's elementary schools and the principals, who are working so selflessly on behalf of children.

I would like to close with what my grandfather would have called a benediction. On a very personal level, I should like to say that I am most grateful to God for the help I felt in completing this report during a time of illness. My concern now is not to have another Carnegie report discussed by the critics or even by those who praise it, but rather to continue to stir ideas that might help children, especially the least advantaged.

Ultimately, the aim of the Basic School is not just to build a better school, but, above all, to build a better world for children. It is our deepest hope that not a single child, let alone a whole generation of children, should pass through the schoolhouse door unprepared for the world that lies before them. And there is, we believe, an urgency to this effort. Chilean poet Gabriela Mistral wrote: "Many things we need can wait. The child cannot. Now is the time his bones are being formed, his blood is being made, his mind is being developed. To him we cannot say tomorrow, his name is today."

Responding to this challenge is, in the end, what the Basic School is all about.

High School: Thoughts on the Great Debate of 1983–84

Association for the Advancement of International Education
San Diego, California
February 21, 1984

FOR EDUCATORS, 1983 and 1984 were vintage years. After more than a decade of neglect, education became a top priority again. It was nearly everybody's candidate for reform. Thirty governors organized task forces on the schools, as did counties and school districts, superintendents and school boards. Whatever the eventual outcome of all of this upheaval, it's clear that education in America is not now being ignored, not merely taken for granted, nor mindlessly condemned. This is an achievement.

Education matters once again.

One encouraging development has been the renewed commitment of business and higher education leaders to public education. The heads of corporations and presidents of our most prestigious universities have been speaking out for public education. And, once again, school-college collaboration is in vogue. In 1981, the first summit meeting between state chief education officers and college and university presidents convened in Colorado. A follow-up conference was convened at Yale University in 1983 and, thanks to a grant from the Andrew W. Mellon Foundation, school-college projects are now being supported in states from coast to coast.

I have also been especially impressed by the turn-around in the public attitude toward teachers. For decades teachers have been portrayed as ill-prepared, self-serving people who cared less about students than about salary increments, "perks," and privileges. Suddenly, teachers are being presented in a more realistic, more sympathetic light.

While there are inept teachers in the public schools, we are beginning to understand that concentrating only on the weakest teachers misses an essential point. We are beginning to see that whatever is wrong with America's public schools cannot be fixed without the help of teachers already in the classrooms. Most of them will be there for years to come, and teachers must be viewed as part of the solution, not the problem.

For almost twenty years almost every education debate began and ended with talk about the budget. Now, however, we have settled down to a more thoughtful, constructive discussion about how to improve the working conditions of teachers and how to honor outstanding teachers. There is growing agreement—and this is a real achievement—that the time has come to reaffirm the centrality of teaching, to support good teachers and give them the recognition they deserve.

And there is a renewed commitment to the purposes of education. We debated more about money than about ideas, and I dreamed of the day when the goals and content of education might be discussed before we focused on the budget.

That day arrived. During 1983, audiences—for at least that fleeting moment—were eager to discuss educational excellence and how it can be achieved, without turning immediately to the cost.

In the 1983 Carnegie report, *High School*, we declare that "the first essential step for school excellence is a clear and vital mission." High schools, we said, must have a sense of purpose, with teachers, students, administrators, and parents sharing a vision of what they are trying to accomplish. This vision must be larger than a single class in a single day. It must go beyond keeping students in school and out of trouble and be more significant than adding up the Carnegie units the students have completed.

The renewed focus on curriculum is another encouraging development. For the first time in several decades, what we teach in school is being thoughtfully re-examined. There is a growing recognition that what is taught is what is learned and that to be prepared to live in our interdependent, complex world, students must be well informed.

But as I see it, two different positions are being pushed in the current curriculum discussions. One has to do with a humanistic approach to education and its outcomes. The other has to do with an economic approach with emphasis on the nation's competitive advantage in the so-called "high tech" race.

At the moment both approaches appear to be working generally in the same direction. But the long term consequences for education surely will be different depending on which one prevails. In the Carnegie report, for example, we urge the mastery of language which we define as the "basic of the basics." And in our proposed core we urge a curriculum in which all students are introduced to those sequential ideas, experiences, and traditions common to all of us by virtue of our membership in the human family.

In the great education debate of 1983–84, leadership also has been reaffirmed. For years now, studies have pointed to the pivotal role of the principal in bringing about more effective schools. Our own field studies bear out these findings. In schools where achievement was high and where there was a clear sense of community we invariably found that the principal made the difference. Like a symphony orchestra, the high school must be more than the sum of the parts. We are recognizing, once again, that if excellence is to be accomplished, strong leadership will be needed to pull the separate elements together in the school and make them work.

At a still deeper level, the debate in the early eighties revealed some rather remarkable and widely-shared assumptions. The various reports reaffirmed that education is essential for all students and that it must be lifelong. These themes keep cropping up time and time again. And there is the repeated affirmation that we can have, in this nation, *equality* and *excellence* as well. It is an audacious claim, a courageous goal, and we should be heartened to find that the people are unwilling to surrender it.

Perhaps the *Paideia Proposal* says it best: "A democratic society must provide equal educational opportunity not only by giving to all its children the same quantity of public education—the same number of years in school—but also by making sure to give all of them, all with no exceptions, the same quality of education." This goal was first stated by John Dewey in *Democracy and Education.*

In our own report we say that the struggle for equity in the schools must not be seen now as a chapter in American history but, rather, as a continuing part of our unfinished work. To push for excellence today without continuing to push for access for less privileged students is to undermine the crucial but incomplete gains that have been made. Equity and excellence cannot be divided.

Finally, the current debate about our schools has revealed, at its core, a remarkable confidence that the "system" will respond. The American "can do" spirit has been reaffirmed—this in spite of dramatic talk of "unilateral disarmament" in education and a feeling conveyed by some reports that the patient was near death.

Still, the general mood can be characterized as upbeat—the message hopeful. Here is one example taken from *A Nation at Risk*, the 1983 report by the National Commission on Excellence in Education: "Despite the obstacles and difficulties that inhibit the pursuit of superior educational attainment, we are confident with history as our guide, that we can meet our goal."

One is left with the uneasy feeling that perhaps some of these affirmations have been made to reassure the readers—and the authors, too. Still the fact that this nation at this unsettling time chooses to live by its hopes—and its resolve—rather than by its doubts is, in itself, a remarkable achievement.

But there is also a dark lining to the silver cloud. At the top of my list is the failure of most reports to confront adequately the crisis facing the most disadvantaged students. During our own study of the high school, I was deeply troubled that some of our public schools seemed to differ from the others not just in *degree*—but in *kind*. The social pathology at these institutions appeared to be so great and the problems so complex that our proposals may not, I felt, be an adequate response. Failure with these institutions has a devastating impact not only on their students, but on their classrooms and teachers, and on the nation.

Again, the problems seem so complex—the breakup of the home, the community wrenched by crime, the lack of motivation, the loss of hope. How, I wonder, and in what ways can the schools appropriately intervene?

In *High School*, we talk about the importance of the early mastery of language, the need for more counselors, more parental participation in the schools, and more support for education in the home. We propose more flexible scheduling arrangements, so students can work and go to school, so students can learn at their own pace, so that reinforcement and affirmation will accompany the student's efforts. Yet, I am still left with an uncomfortable feeling that our proposals fell short of being an adequate response to the compelling need.

My second disappointment is the way we have ignored the tough questions of testing and evaluation. I'm most disturbed that the SAT is still accepted blindly as an adequate report card on the nation's schools—an error promoted by Secretary Bell when he released, with much fanfare, state-by-state SAT comparisons. In the Carnegie report we call for a new test, the Student Achievement and Advancement Test (SAAT) to help *all* students make the transition to work and further education.

I'm also troubled by the inclination of many of the reforms to focus on "the system" rather than the school itself. Reports by national and state commissions can highlight problems and possibilities. State legislators can define teacher requirements and minimum academic standards. But, in the end, the struggle for quality will be won or lost in thousands of classrooms, in the quality of the relationship between the teachers and the students. Simply stated, schools have less to do with "standards" than with people, and it is a disappointment that teachers and students are not adequately involved in the current push toward school reform.

I'm also unhappy by the lack of serious debate about the art of *teaching* and the scandalous fragmentation between the theorists, the researchers, and the practitioners in education. It's more than superficial separation—it's deep suspicion and sometimes confrontation. I suspect that the profession of education is in such a troubled state in part because of this division, because of our inability to move from school to campus to laboratory and back again with the credibility and respect—as one can do in medicine, in business, or in law. In these professions, "practitioner" is not a dirty word.

I have one example from the medical profession that may be useful to those of us in education. I spent one year as a post-doctoral fellow at the University of Iowa hospital doing research in my special field of hearing and deafness pathology rehabilitation. My collaborator was an otolaryngologist who did surgery on the middle ear. Dr. Kos was on the staff at University Hospital; he taught interns. He had a private practice in Iowa City. He worked with me on a study of the success rate of an exotic surgical procedure and, on top of all this, he traveled to national conventions to present progress reports to his colleagues.

It is, I believe, precisely this interplay between theory, practice, research, and professional development that keeps most medical professionals alive and fresh, and it is the *absence* of such interplay that has, I believe, kept education so anemic. To put it simply, I believe most education conferences would be enriched if we could hear the voices of teachers more often than we do currently.

While stating disappointments, I must add to the list the search for easy bromides. There is still an inclination to believe that we can improve schools with a "miracle drug" or two—a longer school year, merit pay. Do the American people, I wonder—from legislators to teachers, from parents to writers of education reports—understand the scope and intensity of the reform endeavor now started? And, have they any sense of the effort and time (as well as the cost) of bringing it to pass?

This problem of easy bromides has been enormously compounded by the lack of leadership in Washington. Secretary of Education Terrell Bell has supported education, but, when *A Nation At Risk* was released, the President talked about prayer in schools and tax relief for parents with children in privately-funded institutions. He then pushed merit pay. At an Indianapolis Forum in December, 1983—a kind of grand finale for the National Commission—President Reagan declared that we don't need more money—we need more *discipline* in the public schools.

This emphasis is consistent with the programs of an administration that, for two consecutive years, sought to cut federal support for education. And now we have a one-year "breather" before the "real cuts" will be made.

No one claims that federal legislation is the only answer. Still, there are responsible federal steps that can and must be taken to achieve equity and excellence and to serve as a signal for state and local leadership. If the current reform movement begins to flag, lack of clear national leadership must be part of the cause since what we hear today too often trivializes and distorts the issues.

And now I'd like to put the school debate in larger context. While preparing our report, I was struck time and time again by the difficulty of examining the school in isolation. Education is affected by larger trends, forces beyond the classroom and the campus that determine, inevitably, the destiny of our schools. No debate about the nation's schools can be thoughtfully conducted without reference to the larger context within which it carries on its work. Let me cite three nagging worries of my own to illustrate the point.

First, most of the reports of 1983, and much of the subsequent discussion in 1984, ignore or gloss over emerging demographic patterns. The truth is that the students who will populate our schools will be precisely those students who have historically been least well served.

The ethnic and racial composition of young America is changing. While the population as a whole is aging, the youth population among black and Hispanic Americans remains large and will proportionately increase. Minorities now represent 17 percent of the total U.S. population; at the same time they make up more than 26 percent of the total school-age population.

By the year 2000, the United States could be home to the world's fifth largest population of persons of Hispanic origin. Our future as a nation will increasingly be linked to our neighbors to the south. It is for this reason that the Carnegie report suggested that Spanish be a second language taught in all our schools.

Urging all students to study English *and* Spanish demonstrates cultural diversity and encourages the understanding necessary for national unity, as well. I have a sure sense that the success of our schools as well as the integrity of the nation will depend on our capacity to achieve unity with diversity. And I have equal confidence that with clear goals, a sensitive climate and great teaching, our children can be well served by public education.

I am also left with the nagging feeling that we have not just a *school* problem but a *youth* problem in this nation. Indeed, it is startling that students were hardly mentioned in the National Commission's report. Unless Americans start looking at the condition of families and communities, there will be no way to have vitality within the public schools. This is particularly true for schools in inner cities plagued by problems of population dislocation, poverty, unemployment, and crime. There cannot be islands of excellence in a sea of indifference.

Time and time again our researchers heard young people say in one way or another that they felt unneeded and unconnected to the communities of which they are a part. In fact, the school has proven a refuge for many troubled youth. As one student told us: "When my mom and dad separated I thought I'd die. I couldn't study and I felt like I had to cry all day. My English teacher, who I like a lot, stayed after school one day so we could talk. I would have never made it through without her help." Another student told us: "One reason I like my school is because I would rather be at school than at home. I even come to school when I have a cold. The reason is because I get bored at home."

The harsh truth is that school is home for many students. It also is one institution in our culture where it is all right to be young. Here, teenagers meet each other, share hopes and fears, and experiment with growing up. This role for the school will never appear on the report card of the public school unless the old-fashioned category "deportment" is added to the list; and unless we grade the school, not just on academic performance, but also on its sensitivity toward students.

Here, then, is the troubling dilemma: Can we "fix" the schools without dealing with the larger social problems? Can we have a healthy school if students feel confined and uninvolved?

In *High School*, we urge (inadequately, I fear) more home support for schools. We also suggest a service term for students. Our aim is to help young people reach beyond themselves and feel more responsibly engaged, to participate in the communities of which they are a part. To formalize the objective, we recommended that every high school student complete a service requirement—a new "Carnegie unit"—involving volunteer work in the community or at school. The proposed service term should be after school, on weekends and in summer, and we suggest that students themselves should find their own assignments, supervised perhaps by volunteers.

Some argue that we are simply loading one more obligation on the schools—after arguing that schools already have too much to do. Perhaps. Still, excellence in the schools means finding ways to help our children understand that to be truly human, one must serve. And I am left with the troublesome conclusion that we cannot have healthy schools if students do not feel good about themselves or about their place in the larger world.

One final thought nags me as I reflect on the debate of 1983-84. I have an uneasy feeling that the scope of the education debate may be too narrowly defined. The National Commission on Excellence in Education was quite properly dismayed by America's slippage in the high tech race. We have lost, or are losing our competitive advantage. In the words of the Commission: "If only to keep and improve on the slim competitive edge we still retain in world markets, we must dedicate ourselves to the reform of our educational system for the benefit of all—old and young alike, affluent and poor, majority and minority. Learning is the indispensable investment required for success in the 'information age' we are entering."

No one can argue with this crisp, disturbing language. National interests must be served. Still, it's my conviction that our educational vision must be not just national, but global. And I respectfully suggest that the National Commission's report might better have been titled *Nations at Grave Risk*.

In the prologue to *High School* we say that the world has become "a more crowded, more interconnected, more volatile and unstable place." And we conclude that "If education cannot help students see beyond themselves and better understand the interdependent nature of our world, each new generation will remain ignorant and its capacity to live confidently and responsibly will be dangerously diminished."

It's significant that during 1983, in addition to several celebrated reports on education, three other major statements were released. Two of these—one by the Environmental Protection Agency and the other by The National Research Council of the National Academy of Sciences—spoke with remarkable agreement about the so-called "greenhouse effect." Eminent scientists discussed, cautiously and yet with urgency, the global phenomenon involving a gradual warming of the earth's atmosphere through an increase in the amount of carbon dioxide in the air around us. This worldwide changing pattern, which human beings have brought upon themselves, will—responsible scientists predict—change dramatically the quality of life on earth perhaps for our children's children, certainly for our children's children's children. In a more recent report, another group of prominent scientists makes predictions that nuclear holocaust could produce destruction and climatic changes of an even more devastating kind. A worldwide fall of debris and smoke could plunge half of the earth into freezing darkness.

I do not suggest a doomsday or Buck Rogers curriculum for the schools. Nor do I suggest that bull sessions about the future should occupy the day. But I must confess that in the quiet moments before dawn, I wonder how our current push for excellence in education relates to the urgent, awesome issues our students will confront. Will adding more Carnegie units enrich the quality of our students' lives or adequately prepare them for the world they will inherit?

I believe it is possible to build a bridge between 1984 and the year 2000:

- Through language study, students should learn to communicate effectively, responsibly, and learn to evaluate the messages of others.

- Through science and math, students in the nation's schools should confront complicated environmental problems.

- Through studies in government and history and western and non-western studies, students should learn about our own heritage, respect other cultures, and consider ways to live together on planet Earth.

- Above all, students should learn to move across the academic disciplines, to think creatively, and deal thoughtfully with consequential issues, understanding that learning must be measured by the wisdom of its application.

In the Carnegie report we recommend that all students complete a Senior Project, a written report that focuses on a significant issue, one that draws upon the various fields of academic study that have made up the student's program. We are confident that, if education is effective, every student will be able to meet this challenge. It is not too much to expect of an educated person.

For educators, 1983 and 1984 were vintage years. Suddenly, public education moved to the top of the national agenda. Governors, corporate leaders, and college presidents reaffirmed their commitment to public education. Solid progress was made during this time in clarifying goals, shaping the academic core, and giving priority to teachers.

If school progress is to be sustained, we must also increase school budgets, find better ways to educate the most disadvantaged students and accept into the nation's life a new generation of Americans who can enrich our culture.

This nation also must find ways to live more comfortably with its children and acknowledge that parents and other members of the community should be full partners in the processes of education. Above all, we must teach our children not just about the past but about the future— the shadowy lines of which are already beginning to take shape.

Educators are by nature optimistic. And while our push for excellence has just begun, I am confident great strides already have been made and that, working together, we can stay the course.

School Reform in Perspective

Education Writers Association
Boston, Massachusetts
April 16, 1993

IN 1982, EDUCATION WRITERS across the country were doing retrospective stories about the impact a fifty-seven pound Soviet satellite had on the nation's schools. Ted Fiske of *The New York Times* called and asked if I thought we'd have another big educational reform movement like the one that followed Sputnik twenty-five years before. All too flippantly I replied, "No, not unless the Japanese put a Toyota into orbit."

What I had overlooked, of course, was that Toyotas and Hondas were, in fact, orbiting our freeways here on earth. I had failed to calculate how fears of a foreign *military* threat had been replaced by *economic* fears.

Having confessed my failure to get a clear fix on the future, let me try my luck at hindsight and reflect briefly on what's happened since the National Commission on Excellence in Education issued *A Nation at Risk* in 1983. Something worth noting is the fact that ten years after the release of this sixty-five-page government report, school reform is still high on the national agenda—thanks, at least in part, to the vigorous support of corporate leaders.

It's quite remarkable that educational policy in this country has "gone national." For three hundred years, local school control was an almost sacred priority in the nation. And as recently as the 1970s, when I was U.S. Commissioner of Education, the words "national" and "education" simply could not be connected. In those days, if I'd have even whispered the words "national standards" I would have been driven out of town.

Today, this country is more concerned about national outcomes than about local school control. We hear talk of national goals, national standards, national assessment, and, according to Gallup surveys, most people in this country even support the idea of a national curriculum—a position that would have been unthinkable a few short years ago.

Looking back, I've also concluded that what we've had, during the past decade, is, not one, but *three* quite separate reform movements—each with its own definition of the problem, its own leadership and its own priorities.

The first reform effort was an embodiment of *A Nation at Risk.* Leaders of this movement accepted its conclusion that excellence could best be accomplished by strengthening the existing system and that leadership for such renewal could be found *within* the educational establishment itself. What was called for was more basic education, more homework, better teachers, and tighter graduation requirements—along with more support.

As it turned out, this formula matched precisely reform activities going on in North Carolina and Mississippi where Governors Hunt and Winter had already made a clear connection between economic development and education.

Later, Dick Riley, Bill Clinton, Tom Kean, Lamar Alexander, and other energetic governors sparked reform initiatives in their own states—helping to create a crusade that yielded remarkable results.

- Since 1983, high school graduation standards have been raised in 42 of the 50 states, according to an Educational Testing Service study.

- Forty-seven states have introduced new student testing programs— and 39 have some form of teacher evaluation.

- About three-fourths of the nation's high schools adopted stricter attendance standards, 27 percent now assign more homework, and 40 percent have lengthened the school day.

- Since 1983, the number of high schools with no-pass, no-play policies has more than doubled—to nearly 70 percent.

- And during the past decade, average teacher salaries have gone up from about $20,000 annually to nearly $36,000 in 1992—a 22 percent increase above inflation.

In the late 1980s, this state-based push for educational renewal was dealt a severe blow by the recession—with school budgets being cut and tenured teachers losing their positions. But the larger point is that the first reform initiative was led by governors who shared the conviction that public education, with all its problems, still had the capacity and the will to revitalize itself.

Meanwhile, a second reform movement was emerging. This initiative accepted the National Commission's diagnosis of the problem but rejected its prescription for reform, which was considered to be both too timid and too trusting.

President Reagan signaled this alternative approach when he announced, just minutes after *A Nation at Risk* was released, "We'll continue to work in the months ahead for passage of tuition tax credits, educational savings accounts, voluntary school prayer, and abolishing the Department of Education"—a statement that bewildered the assembled crowd since the new report said nothing about these issues.

In a radio address a month before, President Reagan charged that the U.S. Department of Education had soured America's "love affair with education." Later, he accused the National Education Association of "brainwashing America's children." Clearly, the President had concluded that remedies for school renewal must be found outside the system, not within.

Former Secretary of Education Terrel Bell, looking back on this period, put it quite directly: "There was simply no commitment (during the Reagan period) to a federal leadership role to assist the states and their local school districts in carrying out the recommendations of *A Nation at Risk.*"

At first, President Bush seemed to tilt toward the more traditional view of school reform. During the campaign he described himself as "the education President." After the election, Mr. Bush convened the nation's first Education Summit. Soon thereafter, in his second State of the Union message, the President announced six goals for all the nation's schools and quickly organized, with the help of governors, the National Education Goals Panel to monitor progress toward their achievement.

As time went on, however, President Bush voiced increased skepticism about the capacity of schools to renew themselves. He described public education as a "failed system" and declared that, "for too long, we've shielded schools from competition and allowed our schools a damaging monopoly of power." School choice became, for the Bush administration, a central reform strategy and Education Secretary Lauro Cavazos made a strong pitch for "choice" in most of the speeches he delivered from 1989 to 1990.

This push for parental choice proved appealing to some governors and legislators, who were, by the end of the decade, running out of reform ideas—as well as money. In fact, during the past five years, 13 states have adopted some form of choice. They've been joined by several of the nation's largest cities. And the voucher issue, even now, is being battled out in Wisconsin, Maryland, and California.

Finally, in the late 1980s, President Bush created the American Schools Development Corporation to help design new schools for a new century. In the private sector, innovations such as Chris Whittle's Edison project, fitted philosophically into the "break the mold" strategy Bush proposed.

What we've had then, since 1983, are two competing visions of school renewal. One approach, working within the education establishment, sought to achieve change by tightening standards and providing more support. A second approach challenged the existing system, proposing more options based on a competitive, market driven model. In my opinion, the confusion and conflicts created by these differing views of school reform cannot be overstated.

Finally, a third reform movement—actually a whole set of initiatives bundled into one—was being led by individual educators and social activists who, for the most part, accepted the more conservative vision of school renewal—even though their proposed remedies differed widely. Looking back, I have identified at least seven separate initiatives within this independent movement.

First, we have had a group of *teacher renewal reformers*, who have insisted that excellence in teaching is the key to school improvement. John Goodlad, for years, has been a vigorous advocate of this essential theme. In The Carnegie Foundation report, *High School*, we called for more dignity and more status for teachers; two reports in the mid-80's—one by the

Carnegie Forum and the other by the Holmes Group—also gave priority to teachers, while the newly established National Board for Professional Teaching Standards worked to establish a nationwide credentialing system.

A second group might be appropriately described as *student-centered reformers*, those who have insisted that effective student learning is the central issue and that bureaucracy, centralization, and standardized testing are barriers to renewal. Ted Sizer, an advocate of this position has, with his Coalition of Essential Schools, focused on creative classrooms, more flexible curricula, teacher autonomy, and less rigid class grouping.

Third, we've had a handful of *curriculum reformers*. E. D. Hirsch in his book, *Cultural Literacy*, powerfully pressed the point that the lack of a core of common learning explains, in large measure, the failure of our schools. Diane Ravitch has also written thoughtfully about the need for more curriculum coherence. Bill Bennett's books, *James Madison High School* and *First Lessons*, set forth, with great precision, what all students should be learning.

Fourth, during the past decade, a small, but growing band of *school equity reformers*, led by Jonathan Kozol, focused on school finance, describing the outrageous funding gap between privileged and poor districts. Meanwhile, school aid formulas in more than a dozen states were declared unconstitutional by the courts. And, even now, the issue of public school funding is being judicially debated in about 30 states.

Fifth, a group of *school restructuring reformers* has called for a more flexible, more decentralized governance for the nation's schools. Al Shanker repeatedly has urged schools to shift from the old industrial model—with its fifty minute periods—to a more flexible scheduling design. Meanwhile, Dave Hornbeck and others helped restructure Kentucky's education system by moving decision making to the local level and holding schools accountable for outcomes, not procedures.

Sixth, a group best described, perhaps, as the *social crisis reformers* concluded that schools cannot be renewed in isolation. We simply must look at the needs of high-risk families—and most especially at children. In response, Jim Comer's network of schools brings comprehensive services to young students. Our own Carnegie report, *Ready to Learn: A Mandate for the Nation*, called for a national strategy to assure that all children are well prepared for school.

Most recently we've had the *national assessment reformers.* Chester Finn, a vigorous advocate of this position, has argued persuasively that students should be required to pass national examinations in basic subjects with high, uniform standards. Meanwhile, experts such as Lauren Resnick and Marc Tucker have been working on new evaluation tools, while the National Academy of Sciences, and other professional associations, contracted with the federal government to develop discipline-based standards.

In summary, the school reform movement of the 1980s was actually characterized by three quite separate forces—state-based, Washington-led, and independent efforts. Taken together, they offered up a rich menu of renewal strategies. However, these efforts have been disconnected and, looking back, I'm convinced the reform movement would have been far more productive if we would have had a forum where various leaders could regularly meet together, sharing insights.

In the end, however, what really matters are not the proposals or experimental projects, but the actual learning that's occurred. Just what evidence is there that the academic performance of students has improved since 1983?

Last week, a national study of student performance in mathematics showed gains in half the states. In reporting this story, one headline read: "Students in Many States Raise Math Scores Steeply." Another read, "Small Improvement Seen in U.S. Students Math Ability." Both were right, of course. Gains were made. But the problem is that we have no agreed-upon "Dow Jones average" to monitor the overall health of education. As a result some analysts view the glass as half empty—others as half full.

On the down side, the composite ACT score is practically unchanged since 1983. That's true of the SATs as well. And the National Assessment of Educational Progress, perhaps our best source, reports that students remain weak in writing, in reading comprehension, in science, and in civics.

On the bright side, we've had modest gains in math, and minority students have shown considerable progress in most subject areas, while still lagging behind their white counterparts.

But there's a deeper problem. To look only at *overall* school performance masks enormous discrepancies just below the surface. It's my own feeling that perhaps 15 to 20 percent of the nation's schools are doing very well. Consider, for example, that since 1982, nearly 2,000 public schools have received national recognition for excellence from the U.S. Department of Education.

At the same time, perhaps 30 to 40 percent of our schools range from good to mediocre—while at least a third or more are in desperately bad shape. These schools have, all too often, been bypassed by reformers—and yet it's here that the problem is most acute. The Carnegie report, *An Imperiled Generation*, declares, "The failure to educate adequately urban children is a shortcoming of such magnitude that many people have simply written off city schools. . . . We find it disgraceful that in the most affluent country in the world so many of our children are so poorly served."

Well, where does all of this leave us?

While we've had constructive action, and while some schools are succeeding and others hold their own, overall we have made only limited progress toward genuine reform. No one can conclude that the overall performance of public education in this country is adequate for the century ahead.

What's missing is a unifying vision of school renewal. In the decade of the 90s, we simply must find ways to set priorities. I suggest that we focus, with special urgency, on two of the nation's six education goals, both of which have wide support.

Specifically, let's embrace the first education goal and work aggressively to assure that all children come to school well prepared to learn. Excellence in education begins before school, even before birth itself, and yet, according to a Carnegie Foundation survey of kindergarten teachers, 35 percent of the nation's children came to school last year linguistically, physically, and socially ill-prepared. School readiness is an urgent mandate for the nation and if our youngest, most vulnerable children are neglected, excellence in education simply cannot be accomplished.

I also propose that special emphasis be given to the third education goal which calls for the assessment of students in basic subjects.

Critics worry, quite correctly I believe, that the national standards and assessment movement could impose rigid testing on all schools and suffocate reform. On the other hand, such an effort, properly directed, could give the reform movement precisely the focus that's been lacking.

The national assessment effort could, for example, drive us back to the curriculum itself. It's one thing to talk about assessing students—but what precisely do we plan to measure? I urgently hope that we can move beyond the old Carnegie units and create, for the twenty-first century, a more coherent, more integrative course of study.

National assessment also should surely lead to the creation of a new generation of evaluation instruments that reflect more accurately the full range of human potential that Howard Gardner so vividly describes in his pathbreaking book, *Frames of Mind*.

Further, national assessment may force us to look more closely at teaching and at learning. After all, the goal of such evaluation should be to help all students succeed, not fail. This means having both *achievement* standards as well as *delivery* standards that hold schools accountable, not just students.

Finally, national assessment could even force us to examine school finance. After all, it's difficult to defend common outcomes if equality of resources is denied.

So, in an intriguing way, the national standards and assessment movement could, if well guided, serve as the fulcrum of reform by focusing the debate on issues at the very heart of education.

To give direction to this ambitious effort, I'd like to see a congressionally-chartered panel established, comprised of distinguished leaders from education, business, and politics, with parents and students, too. In a 1989 speech at the Business Roundtable I suggested that since we have a Council of Economic Advisors, why not have a blue ribbon council to monitor the educational progress of the nation?

I'd like to end with one very personal observation. In Japan, where my granddaughter went to school, the term "sensei"—teacher—is a title of great honor. When all is said and done we simply must make teaching in this country an honorable profession—since it's in the classrooms of America where the battle for excellence, ultimately, will be won or lost.

A Nation at Risk contained this warning: "History is not kind to idlers." It's clear to me that time is running out and that, in the coming decade, our reform efforts simply must become more focused and more effective.

As a general rule I'm optimistic, especially before lunch, and without being too sentimental, it may be worth recalling that *A Nation at Risk*, with all of its headline-making hyperbole, ended on this optimistic note: "Despite the obstacles and difficulties, we are confident that we can meet our goal. We are the inheritors of a past that gives us every reason to believe that we will succeed."

I'd like to believe that before the next decade of reform has been completed this prediction, finally, will come true.

COLLEGES AND UNIVERSITIES

A College of Quality

Association of American Colleges
74th Annual Meeting
Washington, DC
January 14, 1988

THIRTY YEARS AGO this month John Hannah, then president of Michigan State University, delivered the keynote address at the annual meeting of the Association of American Colleges. The Soviets had just hurled a silver ball called Sputnik into space and President Hannah spoke in almost apocalyptic terms. No event in recent centuries, he said, seems even remotely comparable to Sputnik, "save perhaps the discovery of America."

Hannah concluded that higher education's proper response to Sputnik was not only technological; it was humanistic, too. "College graduates," Hannah said, "can face the world of tomorrow only by planting one foot firmly on the solid rock of vocational competence and the other on the rock of moral conviction." So standing, Hannah concluded, tomorrow's graduate is not likely to be swept away by "the torrent of change" sure to come.

This leads me to the central theme of my remarks tonight. I'm convinced that undergraduate education in America does, as President Hannah declared, have two essential missions. The first is to prepare students to live independent, self-sufficient lives, giving them the skills they need to become "vocationally competent," to use John Hannah's formulation. And on this point, higher education, historically, has been doing very well, indeed.

Some years ago, when I was on sabbatical in England, I read C. P. Snow's *The Masters.* In the epilogue of that fascinating book, which deals with the politics of higher education, Snow gives a brief history of Cambridge University in which he tells how, in the twelfth century, young men came to study with a colony of clerics who had assembled along a little river called the Cam. The students lived in poverty, slept on straw, went without food;

it was a dreary life. Snow then asked why did these young men live under such dire conditions to struggle for an education? They did it, he said, for one essential reason: They wanted jobs. They wanted jobs in the royal administration, jobs in the courts, jobs in the church, jobs in the schools. The purpose of education in those days was vocational, Snow concluded.

The point is that education has always been considered useful—and, as we all know, that priority persists today. In 1984, when we asked undergraduates to define the essential outcomes of a college education, "training for an occupation" was at the top. And Alexander Astin's most recent data show that "making money" is a key reason 71 percent of today's students say they go to college, the highest ranking that purpose has received in twenty years. I'm suggesting that all students, regardless of their major, are preparing for productive work—be it engineering, business, history, or English. The assumption of all education is that learning will be directed toward constructive ends and I'm convinced that colleges should support students in their determination to be useful, self-sufficient, and productive.

But what about the moral conviction of which John Hannah spoke? Students want job security and, like the rest of us, they are concerned about careers. But undergraduate education, at its best, also is a time when students search for identity and meaning. And in an era when careerism dominates the campus, is it too much to expect students to go beyond their private interests, learn about the world around them, develop a sense of civic and social responsibility, and discover how they can contribute to the common good? But in our hard-edged, fragmented world, how is this to be accomplished?

I.

I am convinced that the search for a larger more integrative view of education means first that colleges should develop a curriculum with coherence.

The debate about what constitutes legitimate content for undergraduate education is not new. As far back as 1829, Professor A. S. Packard at Bowdoin College called for a course of study that was, as he put it, comprehensive. (Incidentally, it was Packard who first introduced the term "general education" into the curriculum debate a century and a half ago.)

In 1869, Charles Eliot opened the curriculum to electives. In his inaugural address, Eliot summarized what he called "the full range of academic subjects" and told the Harvard faculty: "We will have them all."

Forty years later, when Lawrence Lowell became president of Harvard, he introduced the so-called "distribution requirements" as a compromise between the rigidity of the core and the randomness of electives.

During the tumultuous twentieth century, we have had two great general education revivals—one following World War I and the other after World War II, which was sparked by the powerfully influential Harvard report *General Education in a Free Society*.

In the 1960s, curriculum debates were often too angry and too shrill, but occasionally there was integrity in the encounters. In the 1970s, as concerned academics sought to make the undergraduate experience both intellectually rigorous and personally authentic, many colleges and universities refurbished their general education sequence, but the reforms of that decade frequently reflected a move by faculty to reclaim academic turf rather than define a more intellectually compelling way to educate the students.

Today, general education is, once again, a topic for debate. And this time the discussion seems to be more vibrant than any I have heard in thirty years. The search for a core of common learning now occurring on many campuses today is being pushed, I believe, by the school reform movement and it's also being prodded by the cultural literacy debate occurring in society at large.

But is there, in fact, a knowledge appropriate for all students? And if so, how should it be defined? In the Carnegie report, *College*, we say that all students should above all become proficient in the written and spoken word. We say that all college freshmen should complete a course in expository writing, since it is through clear writing that clear thinking can be taught. The only way I know to teach critical thinking is to have the student reveal what is in his or her mind, either orally or in writing. We urge that writing be taught in every class, whether it is business, science, literature, or mathematics, and, incidentally, mathematics is itself a universal symbol system that's understood all around the world.

We also suggest that all seniors, before they graduate from college, be asked to write a paper on a consequential topic, which, in my opinion, is the best college assessment instrument I know. There is a lot of talk these days about how college students should be evaluated, and I suggest that every student write a senior paper to see whether they can integrate ideas and relate them to some issue of great consequence.

We also suggest that all colleges introduce what we call a senior colloquium series, a modern version of the old-fashioned declamation. Up to a hundred years ago, one earned a college degree, not by turning in green stamps to the registrar; it wasn't accumulated units. In earlier years, students had to prepare a paper and then stand for declamation; that is, somebody cross-examined them. I wonder if we couldn't have a mini-version of the old-fashioned declamation in which perhaps a half dozen members of the senior class, who have already written their papers, would be asked to participate in an open series such as this to present their writing orally in a public forum.

Beyond essential language skills, we also suggest a course of study that would introduce all students to our Western heritage, our social institutions, to science, literature, mathematics, and the arts in order to achieve cultural literacy, to use E. D. Hirsch's helpful formulation. We also say that, to be truly educated, students must go beyond isolated facts and gain a more coherent view of knowledge and a more integrated view of life.

Albert Einstein once wrote that religion, art, and science are branches of the same tree. Frank Press, the president of the National Academy of Sciences, captured this same spirit when he recently suggested that scientists are, in some respects, artists, too. Press observed that the magnificent double helix, which broke the genetic code, was not only rational, it was beautiful as well.

Barbara McClintock, the Nobel Prize-winning geneticist, said to me recently that "everything is one." There is, she said, no way to draw a line between things. (I wonder if Dr. McClintock has looked at a college catalogue in recent years.) And when the physicist, Victor Weisskopf, was asked, "What gives you hope in troubled times?" he replied, "Mozart and quantum mechanics."

Today, in almost every academic field, researchers are asking questions that do not fit into the traditional academic boxes. Indeed, the most exciting scholarship is in "the hyphenated disciplines"—in bio-physics, in psycho-linguistics, and the like. The groundbreaking work is occurring in what Michael Polanyi has called "the overlapping academic neighborhoods."

But where in the college experience do students encounter connections such as these? Where in the grab bag of distribution courses do undergraduates go beyond the separate disciplines, gain perspective, and discover integration?

As I look toward the year 2000, it seems quite clear to me that debates in the larger cultural context will inevitably shape conversations on the campuses. We live in a world that is economically, politically, and environmentally at risk. The protective ozone layer is endangered, our shorelines are polluted, and tropical rain forests are being depleted at the rate of about 100,000 square kilometers per year. And I'm convinced that increasingly scholars will be searching for a more integrated view of knowledge and a more integrated, more authentic view of life. But I worry that at the very moment the human agenda is more global, education in this country is becoming more parochial.

And I am especially disturbed by our neglect of non-Western cultures. During our study of the American high school, we discovered that only two states required a course in non–western studies. In December, Secretary of Education William Bennett proposed a model curriculum for high school, and non–western cultures were barely acknowledged. And in 1984, when we surveyed 5,000 undergraduates, 30 percent said they had *nothing* in common with people in underdeveloped countries. Not one thing in common? What *are* we teaching in our colleges and schools?

Several years ago, my wife, Kay, and I left JFK airport in New York and soon found ourselves in the jungles of Belize. We were there to visit our son Craig and his new Mayan wife. We had, within a few short hours, traveled a thousand miles and a thousand years. At first, I was convinced that the cultures could never be connected; the distances were too great. The urban jungle and the Mayan jungle could not meet.

But as we sat around the open fire, the embers dying, I discovered that so-called "diverse people" do, in fact, have many things in common. At the most fundamental level, we share the universal experiences of birth and growth and death. (Incidentally, two years later, Kay, who is a certified nurse-midwife, delivered our first Mayan granddaughter in that jungle.)

That evening, I also discovered that, whether we are from Belize or Princeton,

- We all communicate; we depend on the symbol system we call language.

- We all recall the past and anticipate the future, and so far as we know, we humans are the only creatures on the planet with the capacity to place ourselves in time and space.

- Further, we are all, regardless of our culture, members of groups and institutions—the Mayans have, in fact, a very well-ordered sense of community and control.

- We all have a love of the aesthetic; the Mayans had art a thousand years before white men "discovered" this continent.

- We all produce and consume. My son's father-in-law spends his day planting and harvesting. After some difficulty, I explained that I spend my time carrying paper and catching airplanes. He looked at me with some bewilderment and asked, "You call that work?"

- And, finally, I discovered that we are all guided by values and beliefs.

What I am suggesting is that these experiences are found among all people and that, despite our diversity, there is, in fact, a shared agenda. And, I'm convinced that it is a central obligation of our colleges and schools to help create within the minds of our young students an understanding of the human commonalities and the interdependency of our world.

But how should this reality be converted into a curriculum for students? There are many ways, of course; let me suggest just one. Two years ago, I read a front-page story in the *Christian Science Monitor*, on the International Council on Monuments and Sites. The report listed 165 special places on earth that the council had identified as of universal value to humankind. These sites and monuments included the pyramids of Egypt, the palace of Versailles, Cuzco in Peru, Persepolis in Iran, the Katmandu Valley in Nepal, and the old walls of Jerusalem, to name just a few.

As I read this fascinating list, I thought: Wouldn't these priceless treasures provide a marvelous framework for an international curriculum for our colleges and schools? After all, we teach our students about the wars the world has waged. Could we also introduce them to the exquisite monuments and sites that celebrate the human spirit and mark our passage on this planet? Would it be possible, I asked myself, for all students, during their twelve or sixteen years of formal schooling, to look not just at the monuments, but also to learn about the people and traditions that produced them? And would it be possible for every student to understand that this generation has a sacred obligation not to desecrate these monuments that so exquisitely mark the human passage on earth?

I am suggesting that quality in undergraduate education means giving students a perspective that is global. And that in the end, the future of the human family will be made secure not by putting weapons systems into space, but by building better human understanding here on earth.

II.

Before leaving the curriculum, I would like to say a word about the major. At most colleges today, there is sharp division between general and specialized education—a two-plus-two arrangement in which students work to get their general education requirements "out of the way" so they can begin their major. Indeed, we observed during our study of the undergraduate experience that students are eager to become competent in specialized fields but what they are *not* asked to consider is: "Competence to what end?"

In the Carnegie report, we suggest that general and specialized education should be blended during college just as, inevitably, they must be blended during life. And to accomplish this objective, we propose *the enriched major.* Under such an arrangement, general education courses would run vertically, from the freshman to the senior year. Departments would teach general education as an extension of the major, and, in a capstone seminar, all students would be asked to put their specialty in historical, social, and ethical perspective.

As the academic major intersects with the themes of common learning, students can return, time and time again, to considerations of language, heritage, social institutions, and the rest.   And when the major is so enriched, students move from depth to breadth and focus not on mere training, but on liberal learning at its best.

Sir Eric Ashby, the noted British educator, wrote: "The path to culture should be through a man's specialism, not by bypassing it. . . . A student who can weave his technology into the fabric of society can claim to have a liberal education; a student who cannot weave his technology into the fabric of society cannot claim even to be a good technologist."

III.

Courses alone do not bring coherence. Integrating the liberal and the useful arts depends every bit as much on people as on programs. Faculty must provide the enlightening and integrative foundation so successful to the undergraduate experience. They also should not only be devoted to their disciplines but also to the embodiment in the classroom of the spirit of a liberal education.

Higher education in the United States draws its inspiration from two great traditions. First, there is the tradition of the colonial college, with its focus on the student, on general education, and on loyalty to the campus. But higher education in this country has also been profoundly shaped by the European university, with its focus not only on the student, but on the professoriate; not on general education, but on specialized knowledge; not on loyalty to the campus, but to the professor.

In our survey of five thousand faculty, we found that 70 percent said their loyalty was to their discipline; 20 percent said their loyalty was to the campus. One professor spoke for many when he said, "My community is the WATS line, not my colleagues down the hall."

But we also found during our research that 60 percent of the faculty surveyed (in a sample drawn from all sectors of higher education) said they prefer teaching to research (in liberal-arts colleges, it was 80 percent), and 60 percent of the faculty agreed that: "Teaching effectiveness, not publication, should be the primary criterion for promotion."

I'm suggesting that there is an enormous ambivalence within American higher education about the division between teaching and research. Somehow, we need to look beyond the "teaching vs. research" cliché and ask the more provocative question, What does it mean to be a scholar?

We should recognize, of course, that scholarship means the discovery of new knowledge, through research. But we also should recognize that scholarship means *integrating* knowledge, through curriculum development. Let us also recognize the scholarship of *applying* knowledge, of finding ways to relate information to contemporary problems. And, above all, let us recognize the scholarship of *presenting* knowledge, through advising and counseling and teaching.

What we urgently need in the academy, then, are scholar-citizens—people who are committed to building an intellectual community, not just in the classroom but in the coffee shop and committee room as well. And until scholarship in American higher education means not only publishing, but also designing integrated courses, serving on committees, and spending time with students, I am convinced that our efforts to renew the undergraduate experience will simply be time spent tinkering on the edges.

IV.

This leads me to another priority in higher education, the building of community and the strengthening of campus life. I do not wish to romanticize the notion of community in higher education. And yet, a college, regardless of its size, must be held together by something more than a common grievance over parking.

In the award-winning Broadway play *Fiddler on the Roof*, the peasant dairyman who raised five daughters says that the things that make life tolerable to the hard-working Jewish family are the old laws and customs. Without these, the dairyman declares, life would be as shaky as a "fiddler on the roof."

So it is with college. While professors teach and conduct research, and while students study on their own, life for most of us is made tolerable by shared rituals and traditions and by our capacity to create community by speaking and listening carefully to each other. Yet, in the rigid departmental structure through which most campuses are governed, we are often so busy pursuing our special categories of knowledge that community is diminished.

Some years ago, our children were playing a record at a decibel level that was calculated to destroy my tympanic membrane. "If you can't turn the volume down," I said, "at least explain to me what I should be enjoying." My daughter brought me the record jacket, and I discovered the Beatles were singing about Eleanor Rigby, a woman who wore a mask she "kept in a jar by the door." And I thought that we in education also wear our masks, often concealing more than we reveal.

Wayne Booth of the University of Chicago once said that, all too often, our inadequate efforts to speak and listen to each other form a vicious cycle, spiraling downward. But Booth went on to say that "we all experience moments when a person's capacity to speak and listen more carefully creates a like response in others." In the end, he said, the spiral can move upward, "leading to rare moments of genuine understanding."

During the 1960s, while Chancellor of the State University of New York, I was preparing to speak to faculty from across the state. It was an especially important moment because the university trustees were there, too. But just as I was to speak, several hundred students moved in with placards, chanting slogans, demanding that I free a group of students in Buffalo who had been arrested the night before. The microphone was grabbed, we argued back and forth.

Finally, after an hour, I concluded that we were not listening to each other. I realized I was talking to a faceless mob. The meeting was in shambles. At that point, I left the platform and walked into the crowd; I began talking to a single student. I asked her name, I asked about her family. Soon, several others joined us. To make the story short, the session ended, a compromise was reached, and, in the process, I came to know some most attractive students.

We hear a lot of talk these days about teaching values in higher education. Frankly, I am not sure this can be accomplished through a separate course in morality or ethics. I am convinced, however, that values are sustained on campus by the honesty of our words, and by the confidence we have in the words of others.

Some years ago, Quakers would risk imprisonment because, in a court of law, they would refuse to swear to tell the truth, the whole truth, and nothing but the truth. In essence, they would say to the judge, "Your honor, I speak truth, and, if I swear it only on a Bible, does that suggest that, outside the courtroom, truth might be an option?"

I am suggesting that in morality there is no place for plausible deniability. If the Iran-contra hearings taught us anything, they taught us that good communication means not just cleverness, not just clarity; it means integrity as well. This, in my judgment, is the key to building community on campus.

V.

Finally, if we are to help students achieve the "moral conviction" of which John Hannah spoke, students must see a connection between what they learn and how they live.

During our study of the American high school, I became convinced that we have not just a *school* problem but a *youth* problem in this country. I become troubled that it is possible for teenagers in society today to finish high school and never be asked to participate responsibly in life, never spend time with older people who are lonely, never help a child who has not learned to read. One student we talked with in Ohio told us that he had a job last summer at McDonald's. "It wasn't very exciting," he said, "but at least I was feeling useful." I think there is something wrong with a society where teenagers define being useful as pushing Big Macs.

Also, there is today an intergenerational separation in our culture. We have created a horizontal layering in which sixteen-year-olds talk only to other young people, and in retirement villages, eighty-year-olds talk only among themselves. We keep young people out of sight, warehoused in schools. Indeed, when we see teenagers on the streets, in groups of more than three or four, we wonder what they are up to.

In our report *High School*, we proposed a new "Carnegie unit." We suggest that all high school students be asked to volunteer to work in hospitals, in museums, in nursing homes, or to tutor other kids at school. A term of voluntary service, whether at the school or college level, could uniquely bind the nation's youth and help them see connections between the classroom and the needs of people.

Martin Luther King once said that, "Everybody can be great because everybody can serve." I am convinced that this nation's young people are genuinely ready to be inspired by a larger vision. All too often, if the headlines are to be believed, the vision we have given them is greed. Could we also suggest that to be truly human one must serve?

Here then is my conclusion. Education must prepare students to be independent, self-reliant human beings. But education, at its best, also must help students go beyond their private interests, gain a more integrative view of knowledge, and relate their learning to the realities of life. This is the meaning of collegiate education.

A Community of Scholars

The Emory Symposium
Atlanta, Georgia
April 14, 1994

I AM DELIGHTED TO BE WITH YOU this evening. Emory University is an institution of world-class distinction, not only because of the scope and quality of its work, but also because of its service to the community. The fact that you have paused, in the midst of a hectic spring, to ask what you are and what you wish to become is, in itself, a testament to the quality of the enterprise that brings us here tonight. And to be here with my colleague Jonathan Cole is a great pleasure. I have respected his outstanding intellectual leadership for years.

Our challenge this evening is to reflect on the choices and responsibilities of the changing university, and to ask quite candidly: What do we wish this university to become in the decade ahead?

Placing our inquiry in larger context, I believe that the most fundamental challenge confronting American higher learning is to move from fragmentation to coherence. If I were to select one term to capture the essence of my remarks this evening, it would be the word "connections"— connections between teaching and research, connections between students, faculty, and staff, connections across the disciplines, and connections from the campus to the larger world. What we need, in short, is a university with a shared vision.

It is also my conviction that achieving more coherence in higher education is accomplished as we examine, with candor, the role of the professoriate, and consider the kind of reward system that should guide the institution in the decade just ahead.

But before looking to the future, I should like to take a backward glance and reflect on how the role of the professoriate has changed throughout the years.

When Harvard College was founded in 1636, the focus was on the student. Teaching was a central, even a sacred, function, and the highest accolade a professor could receive in those days was the famous one that Chaucer extended to the clerk at Oxford when he said, "Gladly would he learn, and gladly teach." Educating the whole person, with a curriculum that was rigidly prescribed, was at the very heart of the colonial college, and for a century and a half, that's what scholarship in America was all about. Even as late as 1869, when Charles Eliot assumed the presidency of Harvard, he declared in his inaugural address that the primary business of the American professor must be "regular and assiduous class teaching."

But change was in the wind and, early in the nineteenth century, the focus of American higher learning slowly began to shift, from the shaping of young lives to the building of a nation. In 1824 Rensselaer Polytechnic Institute was founded in Troy, New York. RPI was, according to historian Frederick Rudolph, a constant reminder that America needed railroad builders, bridge builders, and builders of all kinds. The famous Land Grant Act of 1862 linked higher learning to America's agricultural and technological revolutions, and when social critic Lincoln Steffens visited Madison in 1909, he declared that in Wisconsin "the university is as close to the intelligent farmer as his pig-pen or his tool-house." The curriculum in the nineteenth century, I should add, increasingly shifted from the classics and theology to utility. The regulated core was yielding to electives.

At the turn of the century, David Starr Jordan, the newly appointed president at Stanford, declared that the entire university movement in this country is toward "reality" and "practicality." And on the East Coast, Charles Eliot, still at Harvard, said that "serviceability" is the central mission of higher education. Frankly, I find it amazing that just one hundred years ago the words "reality" and "practicality" and "serviceability" were used by America's most distinguished academic leaders to describe the central mission of higher education in this country. To put it simply, the scholarship of teaching had been joined by the scholarship of building.

Meanwhile, a third vision of scholarship was emerging, a movement that could be traced to the early research laboratories at Harvard and MIT. It was formalized in 1861 when Yale University offered the first Ph.D. ever awarded in the United States. It was further strengthened when American academics who studied at the distinguished German universities of Göttingen and Heidelberg and Humboldt were profoundly influenced by the emerging scholarship of science, with its emphasis on rationality, on meritocrity, and on a curriculum rooted in the empiricism of Isaac Newton.

During the latter part of the nineteenth century, Daniel Coit Gilman, one of the most vigorous advocates of the German model, joined forces with a Quaker philanthropist and in 1876 founded Johns Hopkins University in Baltimore, often referred to as the first true university here in the United States.

At Gilman's retirement in 1896, Woodrow Wilson, who at the time was president of Princeton, described Johns Hopkins as the first university in America where the "discovery of knowledge" was judged superior to "mere teaching." And this may have been the precise moment when the teaching versus research debate actually began, with the discovery of knowledge pitted against something called "mere teaching."

Here I should pause and underscore one absolutely central point. Johns Hopkins, and some other ambitious research universities at the time, remained the exception rather than the rule well into the twentieth century. Most higher learning institutions continued to give top priority to teaching and secondarily to service.

But following World War II, we had a sea change in American higher education. The GI Bill moved us, almost overnight, from "elite" to "mass" higher education, to quote Berkeley sociologist Martin Trow. Thanks to the GI Bill, young men who had served in the war were invited to campus. At that time most academic leaders were nervous about the GI Bill. No longer were students to be admitted only on the basis of ability. Here was an army of eight million coming to college because of their service to the nation. Many worried that these students would lower standards, and one dean of students at a distinguished Midwest university argued that since most GIs were married and would bring baby carriages to the campus, this would plant unwholesome thoughts in the minds of the innocent undergraduates. Well, the GIs did come. They did bring baby carriages. But they also brought experience and energy and focus and dedication.

During this period enrollments exploded, diversity increased, and the undergraduate curriculum moved toward careerism and credentials. The irony was that at the very moment the *social commitments* in American higher learning were being broadened, the *reward system* of the professoriate was being narrowed. While talking about diversity in mission, the academy moved increasingly to a unitary model of academic status. A veritable army of newly minted Ph.D.s invaded campuses from coast to coast, determined to clone the research model that they themselves experienced.

In the early 1960s, I was at the University of California, Santa Barbara, and watched a former teacher training institution being folded into the University of California system. Faculty who were hired to perform one mission were suddenly being held accountable for another, and I saw the confusion of professionals caught in a new paradigm of recognition and reward. I then became Chancellor of the State University of New York, and for seven years we struggled to maintain the separate missions of sixty-four institutions during a time in higher education sociologist David Riesman called the "upward drift," when every institution wanted to be like the one just above it, and so became more imitative than creative.

During this period something else happened of great consequence to higher learning. Because of exponential growth, it was necessary to develop a new kind of governance in what Clark Kerr called the "multiversity," and the California master plan is probably the best example. This new governance structure was built more on the industrial than the collegial model. It was a hierarchy of decision making, with messages moving up and down the line. The horizontal model of collegiality was lost, which led to a breakdown in trust between the faculty and the administration. It's sad that Carnegie Foundation surveys show that about 40 percent of the academy view administrators at their institutions as "autocratic." This suggests to me a breakdown in communication, not necessarily a breakdown in the integrity of the individuals who are administrators.

Thus, by the late twentieth century, the land grant tradition had largely faded from the scene, and most campuses in the United States were caught in the crossfire of the two remaining traditions. On the one hand, there was the colonial college tradition, with its emphasis on the student, its emphasis on general education, and its emphasis on loyalty to the campus. On the other hand, there was the German university tradition, with its emphasis not on the student, but on the professoriate; not on general education, but on specialized education; not on loyalty to the campus, but on loyalty to the guild. We did not find an adequate way to mediate the two. Almost all consequential debates on campus—debates such as teaching versus research, general versus specialized education, the quality of campus life, and service beyond the campus—are really a struggle for the soul of the institution. Are we a colonial college or are we a European university, or a blend of both?

The truth is that most campuses would like to have their cake and eat it, too. When out recruiting students, campuses are collegiate to the core and that's the way viewbooks describe them. Several years ago, I studied carefully thirty viewbooks, which are the marketing devices colleges use to attract students and their parents. Time and time again, I found the words "community" and "caring" and even "family." I also looked at the pictures in these viewbooks. Based upon the pictures, I concluded that about 60 percent of all college classes in the United States are held outside, underneath a tree, usually by a gently flowing stream. One recruiter told a Carnegie researcher, "Water is very big this year."

But when students actually enroll, they discover that instead of being a family, the campus is, in fact, divided into two separate worlds, reflecting two unmediated traditions, with a student (colonial college) culture on the one side, and a faculty (European university) culture on the other. And freshmen and sophomores especially feel like strangers in a foreign land, cared for by "student services" colleagues who are expected to keep the collegiate tradition alive.

When students choose a major, they enter another kind of academic culture, where the faculty and students begin to come together. As they move up the academic ladder to graduate school, the cultures tend to further integrate, and, of course, by the time students are working on the Ph.D., there's an intimate interaction. The cultures at that point have finally blended.

Simply stated, we have in American higher education wonderfully rich traditions—the colonial college, the land grant college, the European university—but we haven't found a way to integrate the separate priorities that have contributed so profoundly to the heritage of higher learning in this country.

What are we to do about all this?

At The Carnegie Foundation several years ago, we prepared a report called *Scholarship Reconsidered*. The purpose of this report was to try to develop a new language that would allow us to achieve a new sense of community and integration around a well-defined mission. We concluded in *Scholarship Reconsidered* that it's time to move beyond the tired old teaching versus research debate and begin to ask the much more intriguing question, "What does it mean to be a scholar?" In response, we proposed a definition of scholarship with four interlocking parts.

We say in our report that the intellectual life begins with what we call the *scholarship of discovery*. We take the position that every member of the academy should demonstrate his or her ability to do research, and we insist that the university continue to be the home of disciplined investigation. Fifty years ago Vannevar Bush, of MIT, a truly remarkable figure during the transition after World War II, said, "Universities are the wellsprings of knowledge and understanding. As long as their scientists are free to pursue truth wherever it may lead there will be a flow of new scientific knowledge." The scholarship of discovery, in my opinion, is at the heart of academic life, certainly at a research center. But in our report, we suggest that the pattern of research within higher learning may vary from campus to campus; it may vary within a university from department to department; and it may vary within individuals from year to year, and even across a lifetime.

Research is only the beginning. In addition to the scholarship of discovery, we say in our report that universities also must give priority to what we call the *scholarship of integration*. It's my own deep belief that discoveries take on meaning only when they're placed in larger context. The problem is not just the divisions among departments and the divisions among students and professors, and divisions between student life and academic life. The problem is also that the interior of knowledge itself has been broken up. We've lost a sense of overall perspective. Fragmentary knowledge seems increasingly to preoccupy the academy.

And yet, research increasingly points to the essential connectedness of knowledge. The work of geneticist and Nobel laureate Barbara McClintock, for example, illustrates clearly that everything is one, that there is no way to draw a line between things. McClintock's research establishes the absolute dependence of variables on each other.

Frank Press, recently retired president of the National Academy of Sciences, delivered a speech several years ago in which he suggested that, in some respects, the artist and the scientist are in fact very much alike. And to illustrate his point, he said that the magnificent double helix, which broke the genetic code, was not only rational, but beautiful as well. When I read this speech, I thought of watching the liftoffs at Cape Kennedy. When the rocket moved successfully into orbit, the scientists and engineers wouldn't say, "Well our formulas worked again." They'd say, almost in unison, "Beautiful!" They chose an aesthetic term to describe a technological achievement.

But where in our fragmented academic world can scholars make connections such as these? Clifford Geertz, at the Institute for Advanced Study, wrote a fascinating monograph several years ago entitled "Blurred Genres," in which he argues that a new paradigm of knowledge is beginning to emerge simply because the old boxes don't fit the new intellectual questions, nor do they fit the new social imperatives that are bringing the disciplines together.

On most campuses, artists and scientists, to say nothing of humanists and engineers, actually live in pockets of isolation, essentially separated from each other, with very little discourse. Academic departments, in my view, in recent years have become political and budgetary bases rather than centers of intellectual quest. I am convinced, however, that the boundaries between the disciplines are becoming blurred, that the cognitive map is changing, and that some of the most exciting work in the academy today is in the new hyphenated disciplines—in psycho-linguistics, bio-engineering and the like.

We need the scholarship of discovery and we need to place discovery in larger contexts, achieving integration among the disciplines. But beyond these, we need what we call in our report the *scholarship of application*. We need to find ways to relate the theory of research to the realities of life.

Historically, higher learning in this country was viewed as a public good. "Princeton in the nation's service," is the way Woodrow Wilson put it at the turn of the century. The colonial college was to prepare civic leaders for the country. The land grant college was to help to build in a more applied fashion. But increasingly today, as I listen to the politicians and the public policy people, and even to the press, the work of higher learning in this country is being viewed as a private benefit and not as a public good. The campus is being considered a place where faculty get tenured and where students get credentialed, but a place that has little to do with the nation's pressing social and economic problems.

Vannevar Bush viewed the university as a place for service to the nation through research and its applications. To put it simply, the university was part of the solution, not the problem. But what's happened today is that the academy is being seen as part of the problem, lined up with all the others asking for assistance, self-serving and turning inward. Many believe that if the students are the main beneficiaries, then they should pay the bill. Student tuition continues to rise at an alarming rate, with virtually no public policy debate or vision about the mission of public learning, no sense that to invest in young people is to invest in the future of the world. It's not because we're low on funds, but because we've lost the vision.

The time has come to create in this country a network of service universities, institutions that respond to the educational and health and urban crises of our day, just as the land grant colleges responded to the needs of agriculture and industry a century ago. This is not simply "doing good." Unfortunately the term "service" has been so diminished, we see it as doing anything that seems to be sentimentally appropriate. I'm drawing a sharp distinction between what I call the civic functions of the academy, that is, doing what you need to do in order to be a good citizen both on and off the campus, and the academic functions of applying knowledge, relating one's discipline and theories to the reality around you. That's quite a different definition of service.

Donald Schön of MIT, in his book *The Reflective Practitioner,* proposes a new epistemology of practice, one in which scholars move not only from theory to practice, but also from practice back to theory. There's increasing evidence that in fact the best way to shape one's theory is in the application of it. The new models of medical education, the new models in law, in engineering, and in architecture, suggest that you cannot remove theory from practice, and that well-defined practice refines theory. So in developing and defining scholarly work, we simply must give new dignity and new status to the scholarship of application.

We say in the Carnegie report that scholarship means not only the ability to discover knowledge, to integrate knowledge, and to apply knowledge, but also in the end it means transmitting knowledge in what we call the *scholarship of teaching*.

Several years ago, I counted all the teachers I had had. I remembered three or four in particular who consequentially changed my life. I remembered a literature professor who read Shakespeare aloud in class and I came to understand that literature is an inquiry into the deepest yearnings of the human spirit.

I remembered Mr. Wittlinger, a high school history teacher, who stopped me one day after class and said, "Ernest, you're doing well in history. You keep this up, you just might be a student." This, the highest academic accolade I'd had, caused me to rethink who I was and what I might become. I remembered my first grade teacher, who, on the first day of school, said to twenty-eight frightened, awestruck, anticipating children, "Good morning, class. Today we learn to read."

Teaching sustains scholarship. Without scholarship as a public act, the continuity of learning is broken. Teaching can take many forms, of course. Publishing in a journal is an act of teaching. A presentation at a conference is an act of teaching.

What's troubling is that, on most campuses, it is far better to deliver a paper at a convention at the Hyatt in Chicago than it is to teach undergraduates back home. What does this say about our priorities? We affirm teaching, but only teaching to our peers. We affirm teaching in distant places, and we affirm teaching through the printed page. But we often fail to give credibility to teaching future scholars in the classroom. Even the language that we use is revealing. We refer to research *opportunities*, and to the teaching *load*.

Robert Oppenheimer, when he spoke at Columbia University many years ago, said, "It is proper to the role of the scientist that he not merely find new truth and communicate it to his fellows, but that he teach, that he bring the most honest and intelligible account of new knowledge to all who will try to learn." And surely this means teaching future scholars in the classroom.

I've suggested that there are four interlocking dimensions to the work of scholarship, beginning with the scholarship of discovery. Research must continue to be the centerpiece of the intellectual life, and our commitment to research must grow, because our problems are growing. But to avoid pedantry, we also must affirm the scholarship of integrating knowledge. And to avoid irrelevance, we need to support the scholarship of applying knowledge. And finally, let's give new dignity and new status to the essential act of teaching, to keep the flame of scholarship alive. Could we create on campuses today a reward system in which all forms of scholarship would be defined and appropriately rewarded?

This new paradigm of scholarship, I believe, holds enormous potential for colleges and universities. With this broader definition, it would be possible for a university to describe with more confidence and courage its own distinctive mission, working out the formulas and the relationships between those forms of scholarship that fit uniquely that particular campus. I believe this new paradigm of scholarship also has meaning for the faculty. Rather than making all faculty into academic clones, could we embrace the full range of talent and make creative use of the diversity of the academy?

And could we also celebrate diversity over a professional lifetime? In our report *Scholarship Reconsidered*, we suggest something called "creativity contracts" in which some faculty might decide that over the next three to five years, for example, they would focus on the scholarship of discovery, doing less teaching. Then for the next several years, they might engage more in the scholarship of applying knowledge. An individual professor would shift the focus several times over many years, allowing for great renewal and growth along the way. Across a lifetime, intellectual interests may shift, and we need to allow for this natural, creative process.

Finally, the redefinition of scholarship might also be appropriate for the students. Why not have all incoming students join with faculty right away as young scholars in the discovery of knowledge, in the integration of knowledge, in the application of knowledge, and in the communication of knowledge? Why not have these four dimensions of scholarship become the four essential goals of undergraduate education?

A new kind of freshman year experience could be created that gets immediately into the interior of the work of the professoriate itself. Senior professors could offer mini-courses during the first semester, meeting with students in a series of two- or three-day seminars to give an overview of the discipline in which they work or describe an exciting research project. Some students might even begin their specialty during the freshman year by identifying the areas of study that interest them.

And rather than having freshmen and sophomores take a grab bag of general education courses for two years—which students and professors alike regard as something to "get out of the way"—why not offer all undergraduates a series of cross-disciplinary seminars that also would run vertically from the freshman to the senior year, running parallel to and perhaps interweaving with the major? These seminars could take up such topics as great events that changed the course of history, or historic landmarks around the world, or a comparative study of five civilizations, or six urgent social problems that need to be confronted. All of these seminars would be taught and guided by faculty from several disciplines, and perhaps at the end of that integrated effort, there might be a capstone seminar which could be connected to the major.

And why not have every undergraduate complete a research project under the tutelage of a professor? Each student could put his or her specialty in historical, social, and ethical perspective. This course of study would take students from breadth to narrowness, and back to breadth again, and students would be introduced to the scholarship of integration.

And, rather than have all undergraduates spend all their time on campus, engaged only with theory, why not have all undergraduates engage in a field experience or a community project as a requirement for graduation, introducing them to the scholarship of application? This would be a serious effort in which students take an idea, apply it, and then evaluate their work, all under the close supervision of professors.

And finally, rather than have undergraduates remain passive in the classroom, why not assume that these young students should in fact be teachers, too, at times, actively engaged in communicating knowledge to their peers? And every student should write a senior thesis to demonstrate an ability to communicate not only accurately, but ethically as well.

The time has come to view all incoming students not as the great unwashed, but as young scholars in the making. If we would develop a common language to allow both faculty and students to engage in the scholarship of discovery, integration, application, and communication, we might close the gap between undergraduates and the professoriate and begin to create a true community of learners on the campus.

Fifty years ago Mark Van Doren wrote that the "connectedness of things is what the educator contemplates to the limit of his capacity." No human capacity is great enough, he said, to permit a vision of the world as simple, but if the educator does not aim at that vision, no one else will. Van Doren concludes by saying that "the student who can begin early in his life to think of things as connected, even if he revises his view with every succeeding year, has begun the life of learning." The connectedness of things is what the great university is all about, and I believe the great university in the coming century will be described as a *community of scholars*.

The Scholarship of Engagement

American Academy of Arts and Sciences
Induction Ceremony
Cambridge, Massachusetts
October 11, 1995

I AM VERY PLEASED to join you at this induction ceremony of the American Academy of Arts and Sciences. I congratulate the new members, many of them friends, and share with you the satisfaction of affiliation with this unusually distinguished association. And I am particularly pleased to share the podium with Jary Pelikan. There is no one I admire more—a dear friend who has a rare combination of brilliant intellect, an insatiable curiosity, an irrepressible sense of humor, and deep compassion, and who throughout his spectacular career has contributed so powerfully to the nation's civic and intellectual life.

Let me begin, then, with a self-evident observation. American higher education is, as Derek Bok once poetically described it, "a many-splendored creation." We have built in this country a truly remarkable network of research universities, regional campuses, liberal arts and community colleges, which have become, during the last half century, the envy of the world.

But it's also true that after years of explosive growth, America's colleges and universities are now suffering from a decline in public confidence and a nagging feeling that they are no longer at the vital center of the nation's work. Today, they are not being called upon to win a global war, or to build Quonset huts for returning GIs. They're not trying to beat the Soviets to the moon or to help implement the Great Society programs. It seems to me that for the first time in nearly half a century, institutions of higher learning are not collectively caught up in some urgent national endeavor.

Still, our universities and colleges remain, in my opinion, one of the greatest hopes for intellectual and civic progress in this country. However, for this hope to be fulfilled, the academy must become a more vigorous partner in the search for answers to our most pressing social, civic, economic, and moral problems, and must reaffirm its historic commitment to what I haven chosen to call, this evening, the *scholarship of engagement.*

The truth is that for more than 350 years higher learning and the larger purposes of American society have been inextricably interlocked. The goal of the colonial college was to prepare civic and religious leaders—a vision succinctly captured by John Eliot, who wrote in 1636: "If we nourish not learning, both church and commonwealth will sink." Following the Revolution in 1798, the great patriot Dr. Benjamin Rush declared that the nation's colleges would be "nurseries of wise and good men, to adapt our modes of teaching to the peculiar form of our government." In 1824, Rensselaer Polytechnic Institute was founded in Troy, New York, and RPI was, according to historian Frederick Rudolph, a constant reminder that America needed railroad builders, bridge builders, builders of all kinds. During the dark days of the Civil War, President Abraham Lincoln signed the historic Land Grant Act, which linked higher learning to the nation's agricultural, technological, and industrial revolutions. And when social critic Lincoln Steffens visited Madison in 1909, he observed that, "In Wisconsin, the university is as close to the intelligent farmer as his pig-pen or his tool-house."

At the beginning of this century, David Starr Jordan, president of that brash new institution on the West Coast, Stanford, declared that the entire university movement in this country "is toward reality and practicality." Harvard's president, Charles Eliot, who was completing his tenure of nearly forty years, said America's universities are filled with the democratic spirit of "serviceableness." And in 1896 Woodrow Wilson, then a forty-year-old Princeton University professor, insisted that the spirit of service will give a college a place in the public annals of the nation. "We dare not," he said, "keep aloof and closet ourselves while a nation comes to its maturity."

Frankly, I find it quite remarkable that just one hundred years ago, the words "practicality" and "reality" and "serviceability" were used by the nation's most distinguished academic leaders to describe the mission of higher learning—which was, to put it simply, the scholarship of engagement. During my own lifetime, Vannevar Bush, of MIT, formally declared, while in Washington serving two presidents, that universities which helped win the war could also win the peace—a statement which led to the greatest federally funded research effort the world has ever known. I find it fascinating to recall that Bush cited radar and penicillin to illustrate how science could be of practical service to the nation. The goals in the creation of the National Science Foundation—which led to the Department of Defense and the National Institutes of Health—were not abstract. The goals were rooted in practical reality and aimed toward useful ends.

In the 1940s, the GI Bill brought eight million veterans back to campus, which sparked in this country a revolution of rising expectations. May I whisper that professors were not at the forefront urging the GI Bill? This initiative came from Congress. Many academics, in fact, questioned the wisdom of inviting GIs to campus; after all, these men hadn't passed the SATs—they'd simply gone off to war, and what did they know, except survival. The story gets even grimmer. I read some years ago that the dean of admissions at one of the well-known institutions in the country opposed the GIs because, he argued, many of them would be married; they would bring baby carriages to campus, and even contaminate the young undergraduates with bad ideas. I think he knew little about GIs, and even less about the undergraduates at his own college.

But putting that resistance aside, the point is largely made that the universities joined in an absolutely spectacular experiment, in a cultural commitment to rising expectations, and what was for the GIs a privilege became, for their children and grandchildren, an absolute right. And there's no turning back.

Almost coincidentally, Secretary of State George C. Marshall, in 1947, at a commencement exercise at Harvard, announced a plan for European recovery, and the Marshall Plan sent scholars all around the world to promote social and economic progress. Ten years later, when the Soviets sent Sputnik rocketing into orbit, the nation's colleges and universities were called upon once again, this time to design better curricula for the nation's schools and to offer summer institutes for teachers. And one still stumbles onto the inspiration of that time. I remember having lunch in Washington one day. We thought we were talking privately about the federal program to help teachers under the Eisenhower administration, only to find we were being overheard at the next table, which you should always assume in Washington. And the man stopped by and said, "I just wanted to tell you that I was one of the NDEA fellows at that time, and I've never had a better experience in my life." And the inspiration of the teachers who came back from the summer institutes touched teachers all across the country. The federal government and higher education had joined with schools toward the renewal of public education.

Then in the 1960s, almost every college and university in this country launched affirmative action programs to recruit historically bypassed students and to promote, belatedly, human justice.

I realize I have just dashed through three and a half centuries in three and a half minutes, more or less. What I failed to mention were the times when universities challenged the established order, when they acted appropriately both as conscience and social critic, and that, too, was in service to the nation. And there were other times when campuses were on the fringes of larger national endeavors, standing on the sidelines, failing to take advantage of opportunities that emerged. Still, I am left with two inescapable conclusions. First, it seems absolutely clear that this nation has throughout the years gained enormously from its vital network of higher learning institutions. And at the same time it's also quite apparent that the confidence of the nation's campuses themselves has grown during those times when academics were called upon to serve a larger purpose—to participate in the building of a more just society and to make the nation more civil and secure.

This leads me then to say a word about the partnership today. To what extent has higher learning in the nation continued this collaboration, this commitment to the common good?

I hope I don't distort reality when I suggest that, in recent years, the work of individual scholars, as researchers, has continued to be highly prized, and that also, in recent years, teaching has increasingly become more highly regarded, which of course is great cause for celebration. But it seems to me that it's also true that at far too many institutions of higher learning, the historic commitment to the scholarship of engagement, as I've chosen to call it, has dramatically declined.

I do a lot of work with colleges and universities, and study countless catalogs, and it won't surprise you to hear that almost every college catalog in this country still lists teaching, research, and service as the priorities of the professoriate. And yet it won't surprise you either that at tenure and promotion time, service is hardly mentioned. And even more disturbing, faculty who do spend time with so-called applied projects frequently jeopardize their careers.

Russell Jacoby, in a fascinating book entitled *The Last Intellectuals*, observes that the influence of American academics has declined precisely because being an intellectual has come to mean being in the university and holding a faculty appointment, preferably a tenured one; of writing in a certain style understood only by one's peers; of conforming to an academic rewards system that encourages disengagement and even penalizes professors whose work becomes useful to nonacademics—or *popularized*, as we like to say. Intellectual life, Jacoby said, has moved from the coffee shop to the cafeteria, with academics participating less vigorously in the broader public discourse.

But what I find most disturbing, as almost the mirror image of that description, is a growing feeling in this country that higher education is, in fact, part of the problem rather than the solution—going still further, that it's become a private benefit, not a public good. Increasingly, the campus is being viewed as a place where students get credentialed and faculty get tenured, while the overall work of the academy does not seem particularly relevant to the nation's most pressing civic, social, economic, and moral problems. Indeed, there follows from that the concept that if the students are the beneficiaries and get credentialed, then let students pay the bill. And I've been almost startled to see that, when the gap increases in the budget, it's the student, and the student fees, that are turned to automatically—after all, it's a private benefit, and let the consumer, as we like to say, pay the bill.

Not that long ago, it was generally assumed that higher education was an investment in the future of the nation—that the intellect of the nation was something too valuable to lose, and we needed to invest in the future through the knowledge industry.

I often think about the time when I moved, almost overnight, from an academic post in Albany, New York, to a government post in Washington,

DC. These were two completely separate worlds. At the university, looking back, I recall rarely having serious dialogues with "outsiders"—artists, or "popular" authors, or other intellectuals beyond the campus. And yet, I was fascinated by Derek Bok's observation, on leaving his tenured post at Harvard, that the most consequential shifts in public policy in recent years have come not from academics, but from such works as Rachel Carson's *Silent Spring*, Ralph Nader's *Unsafe at Any Speed*, Michael Harrington's *The Other America*, Betty Friedan's *The Feminine Mystique*—books which truly place the environmental, industrial, economic, and gender issues squarely in a social context.

I teach occasionally at the Woodrow Wilson School, in the public policy center, and I open the first class by asking, "How is public policy shaped in America? Where does it originate? How does the debate get going?" And almost always the undergraduates will start with the president, then Congress, or they might think of the state legislature. Then I ask them, has anyone ever heard of Rachel Carson, or Michael Harrington, and a kind of bewildered look appears. And yet the truth is that out of the seminal insights of such intellectuals, public discourse begins, and very often Congress is the last, not the first, to act, trying to catch up with the shifting culture. So it is with the academy. One wonders why discourse between faculty and intellectuals working without campus affiliation can't take place within the academy itself.

But, on the other hand, I left Albany and went to Washington, and I must tell you that I found government to be equally, or I'll go one step further, even more startlingly detached. In Washington we did consult, I want to assure you, with lawyers and political pressure groups, driven usually by legislative mandates, and certainly by White House urges. But rarely were academics invited in to help put our policy decisions in historical or social or ethical perspective. And looking back, I recall literally hundreds of hours when we talked about the procedural aspects of our work and the legal implications, but I do not recall one occasion when someone asked, "Should we be doing this in the first place?"—a question which I suspect could only have been asked by a detached participant with both courage and perspective.

Recently I've become impressed by just how much this problem, which I would describe as impoverished cultural discourse, extends beyond government to mass communication where, perhaps with the exception of MacNeil/Lehrer and *Bill Moyer's Journal*, the nation's most pressing social, economic, and civic issues are discussed by politicians and self-proclaimed pundits, while university scholars rarely are invited to join the conversation.

Abundant evidence shows that both the civic and academic health of any culture is vitally enriched as scholars and practitioners speak and listen carefully to each other.   In a brilliant study of creative communities throughout history, Princeton University sociologist Carl Schorske, a man I greatly admire, describes the Basel, Switzerland, of the nineteenth century as a truly vibrant place where civic and university life were inseparably intertwined. Schorske states that the primary function of the university in Basel was to foster what he called "civic culture," while the city of Basel assumed that one of its basic obligations was the advancement of learning. The university was engaged in civic advancement, and the city was engaged in intellectual advancement, and the two were joined. And I read recently that one of the most influential commentators didn't achieve his fame from published articles, but from lectures he gave in the Basel open forum.

I recognize, of course, that "town" is not "gown." The university must vigorously protect its political and intellectual independence. Still, one wonders what would happen if the university would extend itself more productively into the marketplace of ideas. I find it fascinating, for example, that the provocative PBS program, *The Week in Review*, invites us to consider current events from the perspective of four or five distinguished journalists, who during the rest of the week tend to talk only to themselves. And I've wondered occasionally what *The Week in Review* would sound like if a historian, an astronomer, an economist, an artist, a theologian, and perhaps a physician, were asked to comment. Would we be listening and thinking about the same week, or would there be a different profile and perspective? How many different weeks were there that week? And who is interpreting them for America?

What are we to do about all of this? As a first step, and coming back to the academy itself, I'm convinced that the university has an obligation to broaden the scope of scholarship. In a recent Carnegie Foundation report entitled *Scholarship Reconsidered*, we propose a new paradigm of scholarship, one that assigns to the professoriate *four* essential, interlocking functions. We propose, first, the *scholarship of discovery*, insisting that universities, through research, simply must continue to push back the frontiers of human knowledge. No one, it seems to me, can even consider that issue contestable. And we argue, in our report, against shifting research inordinately to government institutes, or even to the laboratories of corporations that could directly or indirectly diminish the free flow of ideas.

But while research is essential, we argue that it is not sufficient, and to avoid pedantry, we propose a second priority called the *scholarship of integration*. There is, we say, an urgent need to place discoveries in a larger context and create more interdisciplinary conversations in what Michael Polanyi, of the University of Chicago, has called the "overlapping [academic] neighborhoods," or in the new hyphenated disciplines, in which the energies of several different disciplines tend enthusiastically to converge. In fact, as Clifford Geertz, of the Institute for Advanced Study, has argued, we need a new formulation, a new paradigm of knowledge, since the new questions don't fit the old categories.

Beyond the scholarship of discovering knowledge and integrating knowledge, we propose in our report a third priority, the *scholarship of sharing knowledge*. Scholarship, we say, is a communal act. You never get tenured for research alone. You get tenured for research *and* publication, which means you have to teach somebody what you've learned. And academics must continue to communicate, not only with their peers, but also with future scholars in the classroom in order to keep the flame of scholarship alive.

Finally, in *Scholarship Reconsidered*, we call for the *scholarship of application of knowledge* to avoid irrelevance. And we hurriedly add that when we speak of applying knowledge, we do not mean "doing good," although that's important. Academics have their civic functions, which should be honored, but by scholarship of application, we mean having professors become what Donald Schön, of MIT, has called "reflective practitioners," moving from theory to practice, and from practice back to theory, which in fact makes theory, then, more authentic—something we're learning in education and medicine, in law and architecture, and all the rest. And incidentally, by making knowledge useful, we mean everything from building better bridges to building better lives, which involves not only the professional schools but the arts and sciences as well.

Philosophy and religion also are engaged in the usefulness of knowledge, as insights become the interior of one's life. Recently I reread Jacob Bronowski's moving essay on science and human values, which, as you recall, was written after his visit in 1945 to the devastation of Hiroshima. In this provocative document, he suggests that there are no sharp boundaries that can be drawn between knowledge and its uses. And he insists that the convenient labels of pure and applied research simply do not describe the way that most scientists really work. To illustrate his point, Bronowski said that Sir Isaac Newton studied astronomy precisely because navigating the sea was the preoccupation of the society in which he was born. Newton was, to put it simply, an engaged scholar. And Michael Faraday, Bronowski said, sought to link electricity to magnetism because finding a new source of power was the preoccupation of his day. Faraday's scholarship was considered useful. The issue, then, Bronowski concludes, is not whether scholarship will be applied, but whether the work of scholars will be directed toward humane ends.

This reminder that the work of the academy ultimately must be directed toward larger, more humane ends brings me to this conclusion. I'm convinced that in the century ahead, higher education in this country has an urgent obligation to become more vigorously engaged in the issues of our day, just as the land grant colleges helped farmers and technicians a century ago. And surely one of the most urgent issues we confront, perhaps the social crisis that is the most compelling, is the tragic plight of children.

In his second inaugural address, President George Bush declared as the nation's first education goal, that by the year 2000 all children in this country will come to school "ready to learn." Yet we have more children in poverty today than we did five years ago. Today a shocking percentage of the nation's nineteen million preschoolers are malnourished and educationally impoverished. One wonders how this nation can live comfortably with the fact that so many of our children are so shockingly impoverished.

This reality may seem irrelevant in the hallowed halls of the academy or in the greater world of higher learning, yet education is a seamless web. If children do not have a good beginning, if they do not receive the nurture and support they need during the first years of life, it will be difficult, if not impossible, fully to compensate for the failure later on.

To start, higher education must conduct more research in child development and health care and nutrition. This, too, is in service to the nation. But I wonder if universities also might take the lead in creating children's councils in the communities that surround them. The role of the university would be to help coordinate the work of public and private agencies concerned with children, preparing annually, perhaps, what I've chosen to call a "ready to learn" report card—a kind of environmental impact statement on the physical, social, and emotional conditions affecting children, accompanied by a cooperative plan of action that would bring academics and practitioners together. James Agee, one of my favorite twentieth-century American authors, wrote that with every child born, under no matter what circumstances, the potential of the human race is born again. And with such a remarkably rich array of intellectual resources, certainly the nation's universities, through research and the scholarship of engagement, can help make it possible for more children to be "ready to learn." Perhaps universities can even help create in this country a public love of children.

As a second challenge, I'm convinced colleges and universities also must become more actively engaged with the nation's schools. We hear a lot of talk these days about how the schools have failed, and surely education must improve, but the longer the debate continues, the more I become convinced that it's not the schools that have failed, it's the partnership that's failed. Today our nation's schools are being called upon to do what homes and churches and communities have not been able to accomplish. And if they fail anywhere along the line, we condemn them for not meeting our high-minded expectations. I've concluded that it's simply impossible to have an island of excellence in a sea of community indifference. After going to schools from coast to coast, I've also begun to wonder whether most school critics could survive one week in the classrooms they condemn. While commissioner of education, I visited an urban school with a leaky roof, broken test tubes, Bunsen burners that wouldn't work, textbooks ten years old, falling plaster, armed guards at the door—and then we wonder why we're not world-class in math and science, or in anything for that matter.

Especially troublesome is our lack of support for teachers. In the United States today, teachers spend on average $400 of their own money each year, according to our surveys, to buy essential school supplies. They're expected to teach thirty-one hours every week, with virtually no time for preparation. The average kindergarten class size in this country is twenty-seven, even though research reveals it should be seventeen.

About a dozen years ago, the late Bart Giamatti invited me to evaluate the Yale-New Haven Teacher's Institute. I was delighted to discover that some of Yale's most distinguished scholars directed summer seminars based on curricula teachers themselves had planned. And incidentally, teachers in that program were called Yale Fellows. I was startled to discover that they were even given parking spaces on campus, which is about the highest status symbol a university can bestow. I'm suggesting that every college and university should view surrounding schools as partners, giving teaching scholarships to gifted high school students, just as we give athletic scholarships, and offering summer institutes for teachers, who are, I'm convinced, the unsung heroes of the nation.

This leads me to say a word about higher education in the nation's cities. It's obvious that the problems of urban life are enormously complex—there are no simple solutions. Cities determine the future of this country. Our children live there, too. And I find it ironic that universities which focused with such energy on rural America a century ago have never focused with equal urgency on our cities. Many universities do have sponsored projects in urban areas—Detroit, Buffalo, New York, Philadelphia, Baltimore, just to name a few. But typically these so-called model programs limp along, supported with soft money. Especially troublesome is the fact that academics who participate are not professionally rewarded. Higher education cannot do it all, but Ira Harkavay, of the University of

Pennsylvania, soberly warns that our great universities simply cannot afford to remain islands of affluence, self-importance, and horticultural beauty in seas of squalor, violence, and despair. With their schools of medicine, law, and education and their public policy programs, surely higher education can help put our cities and—perhaps—even our nation back together.

Here, then, is my conclusion. At one level, the scholarship of engagement means connecting the rich resources of the university to our most pressing social, civic, and ethical problems, to our children, to our schools, to our teachers, and to our cities—just to name the ones I am personally in touch with most frequently; you could name others. Campuses would be viewed by both students and professors not as isolated islands, but as staging grounds for action.

At a deeper level I have this growing conviction that what is also needed is not just more programs, but a larger purpose, a larger sense of mission, a larger clarity of direction in the nation's life as we move toward century twenty-one. Increasingly, I'm convinced that ultimately the scholarship of engagement also means creating a special climate in which the academic and civic cultures communicate more continuously and more creatively with each other, helping to enlarge what anthropologist Clifford Geertz describes as the universe of human discourse and enriching the quality of life for all of us.

Many years ago Oscar Handlin put the challenge this way: "[A] troubled universe can no longer afford the luxury of pursuits confined to an ivory tower. . . . [S]cholarship," he said, "has to prove its worth not on its own terms, but by service to the nation and the world." This, in the end, is what the scholarship of engagement is all about.

CHALLENGES AND CONNECTIONS

A Partnership:
The Schooling of the Teacher

*A National Conference of Chief State School Officers
and College and University Presidents
Yale University
New Haven, Connecticut
February 17, 1983*

THIS NATIONAL CONFERENCE that brings together chief school officers from almost every state, plus the national leadership in higher education, is one of the most significant events in recent education history. I commend Bartlett Giamatti, president of Yale University, Calvin Frazier, Superintendent of Schools in the State of Colorado, and Jack Sawyer of The Andrew W. Mellon Foundation, for their leadership and vision.

In preparing for this conference, The Carnegie Foundation for the Advancement of Teaching asked Gene Maeroff of the *New York Times* to find out what was going on between colleges and schools. Gene's report, which we are releasing here today, suggests that the barriers between secondary and higher education are breaking down and that school–college collaboration is beginning to mean something more than tea and cookies in the afternoon. Indeed, a major new movement is taking place in American education.

For the first time since Sputnik, education leaders are joining together to clarify requirements for college entrance, to more aggressively encourage new kinds of transition arrangements, and to share more widely faculty and facilities, as well. Excellence has, once again, become a common agenda for the nation's colleges and schools. And, it is especially significant that excellence in *teaching* has been chosen as the focus of this conference.

As most of you know, The Carnegie Foundation is conducting a study of the American high school, and we have spent over two thousand hours in schools from coast to coast. One issue is absolutely clear: the quality of education in this nation is inextricably tied to the quality of teaching.

It is also clear, however, that today the teaching profession is imperiled— rewards are few, morale is low, the best teachers are bailing out, and the supply of good instructors is drying up. This teaching crisis is most dramatically revealed in science and mathematics.

- Since 1972, the number of math teachers emerging from college training programs has fallen 79 percent. In science, there has been a drop of 64 percent.

- In 1982, 32,000 classes in science and mathematics which were planned and needed—involving 640,000 students—could not be scheduled for lack of teachers and resources.

- Equally serious is the fact that, in 1981, half of all newly employed science and mathematics teachers were underqualified to teach these basic subjects.

- The Florida Department of Education estimates that, for the next five years, its colleges and universities will graduate only 20 math teachers a year—this in spite of an annual need for 325 such teachers in schools across the state.

- Of 1,444 Los Angeles teachers—grades 7–12—who have at least one period of math daily, 32 percent have neither a collegiate major nor minor in mathematics.

- In 1982, New York State had only 32 college graduates who planned to teach math in junior or senior high school among some 80,000 who graduated.

- And these are not isolated instances. In fact, in 1981, a total of 43 states reported a shortage of teachers in science and mathematics.

What should be the national response to this crisis that will have enormous impact on the economic future and on the security of the nation?

Last month, in his State of the Union message, President Reagan said that if the United States hopes to keep its edge as world leader we must renew our education system.

·   The President then proposed a $70 million "catch up" program for math and science teachers.

·   And the core of the proposal is a $50 million block grant program to retrain—for math and science—unemployed, retired, and new teachers.

I do not wish to diminish the significance of the government's initiative. But I do wonder if we understand the seriousness of the problem we confront. We cannot delude the nation into believing that rebuilding public education will call for less commitment than rebuilding roads and bridges or rebuilding the security of the nation. And yet, the 1984 federal budget calls for a 6 percent reduction in education, overall, while proposing a $30 billion increase in national defense.

Strengthening America's education system is, in my view, a national problem calling for a national response. Still, I was in government long enough to know that Washington cannot and should not do the job alone. Rather, action at *all* levels is now needed. And, in particular, a new school–college partnership is required—one that involves the collaborative leadership of the institutions in this room.

Therefore—in the remaining time—I should like to focus on excellence in teaching, examining specifically science and mathematics which dramatizes the problem we confront. I should also like to highlight the possibilities of increased collaboration between colleges and schools.

First, to strengthen secondary education teaching means improving education long before students arrive at the high school door. It is inadequate for educators to talk about recruiting high school math and science teachers if, in the early grades, students have not been taught the problem-solving skills on which math and science scholarship depends.

- Today, in the United States, elementary school children spend only about 3 3/4 hours on arithmetic every week—and only about 1 1/2 hours on science.

- And the latest National Assessment of Educational Progress reveals that, during the 1970s, the science performance of "high achieving" students actually dropped—2.4 percent for 4th grade, 4.1 percent for 8th grade, and 4.2 percent for 11th grade. The reason suggested was inadequate science teaching in the early grades.

Clearly, excellence in science and mathematics—or in any other subject—means that a solid academic foundation should be laid for every student in the first years of formal education. If this foundation is *not* in place, students will be chronically behind. High school teachers will be forced to spend their time on remedial education and, in frustration, they will leave. And, of course, colleges will continue to be caught in an unending program of remediation.

Given the importance of the early years, I suggest that a more appropriate response to the math–science crisis might be a major increase in Title I support plus, perhaps, collaboration between colleges and schools to develop a science and mathematics proficiency examination to make sure students in the early grades have mastered basic skills.

Perhaps we also need school–college cooperation to identify, more successfully, young students who are gifted in these special fields. Guilford College offers an educational program called "A Month of Sundays." Invitations are extended by the college through local schools for parents to bring their elementary school daughters and sons to a series of introductory courses taught on Sunday afternoons by Guilford faculty.

The cost of the connection between schools and this college is nominal; the benefits for children as well as their parents are considerable; the modest financial supplement for the faculty is appreciated, and the potential benefits for the nation are immense.

Second, to strengthen teaching—especially in high school math and science—two very different strategies are required. At one level, we must have a solid general education program for every student in every one of the twenty-thousand high schools in the nation. This means a core of basic courses to give all students the skills and knowledge needed to understand and to live effectively in a technologically complicated, interdependent world. To teach successfully in such a program calls for a special vision and special skills as well.

Once again, however, this is not a job for the schools alone. Higher education leaders talk a lot about how general education standards have fallen in the schools. And yet, the harsh truth is that colleges themselves are at least partly responsible for this decline. During the past two decades, college admission standards were abandoned at many institutions and graduation requirements were reduced. If colleges expect high schools to develop a core program of general education, then they themselves must decide what it means to be an educated person. And the quality of college teaching must improve.

Indeed, in the spirit of this conference, is it too utopian to suggest that one of the ways to assure a vital partnership is for teachers from colleges and schools to explore together goals and purposes and to work collaboratively to shape a general education sequence for all students?

But a second strategy is needed. In addition to the general education core for every student, schools and colleges also must provide special opportunities for those students—5, 10, 15 percent perhaps—who have a special aptitude in science and mathematics, those who will become the scholars and pioneers in basic and applied research.

· Three years ago, the state of North Carolina established a residential school in science and mathematics. This institution—serving several hundred outstanding students from all across the state—not only provides a basic education but also offers advanced study in math and science.

· Gifted, well-trained teachers have been recruited and the university is involved, as well, making it possible for high school students to begin to work with scholars in the field.

The point is this: It will be impossible for every high school to provide the top teachers and the sophisticated equipment needed to offer advanced study for talented math and science students. Therefore, I suggest the establishment of a network of residential academies all across the nation. Some may be within a densely populated district; others may serve a single state. And, in less densely populated areas, an academy may serve several states. Some of these academies also might be located on a college campus.

Regardless of sponsorship or location, a network of academies should be collaboratively developed by schools and colleges in every state and region and such schools should receive some federal support since, clearly, the vital interests of the nation are at stake.

One further point. While the emphasis here is on science and mathematics, the need for early identification of gifted students and for continuous, high quality, instruction also applies to other fields—especially foreign languages and the arts. Academies may be needed to serve these equally important specialties as well.

This brings me back to teachers. If we want outstanding instructors in science and mathematics—or in any other discipline—recruiting must begin early, it must be sustained, and both schools and colleges must be aggressively involved.

- The Houston School District has a magnet school for prospective teachers—a place where high school students interested in teaching as a career can get a "feel" for the profession and begin to specialize somewhat.

- While all students at the magnet school complete a solid academic program, they also do classroom observation and have the opportunity to work with outstanding professors from local higher learning institutions and other teachers too.

Another point. Schools and colleges also may collaboratively sponsor a summer "prospective teacher" program for gifted high school students. Under such a program, high school instructors would select several of their ablest students who show an aptitude to teach. These students would receive a scholarship to spend a summer term with an outstanding school teacher and college professor who serve as mentors, not only in the discipline of interest, but in the skills of teaching, too. If a pool of such students were selected early and encouraged, teaching prospects for the future would be enormously enhanced. Further, these promising high school students may well be candidates for teacher scholarships once they apply for college.

But to be successful, the climate on the campus must begin to change. There is at many higher learning institutions a shocking bias against teaching in the public schools. We, at The Carnegie Foundation, met one student at an Ivy League institution who made the problem vividly apparent. He said, "We (who select teaching) at this university are under enormous pressure to justify our choice. (Faculty) try to direct us in other ways. And, of course, most of the other students think we are crazy. . . ."

There is, quite frankly a lot of hypocrisy at work when colleges call for "excellence in the school" while spending several hundred million dollars every year recruiting athletes and spending virtually no time or money recruiting future teachers.

To correct this curious imbalance, the nation's colleges and universities should consider giving full tuition scholarships to the top 5 or 10 or 15 percent of their gifted students who plan to teach in public education. Identifying such students is possible, I suggest, only if schools and colleges agree to work together to promote teaching and to mount recruitment programs such as those described. If higher education leaders wish to be part of the solution—rather than the problem—they must speak with conviction about the significance and the dignity of teaching in the public schools.

Excellence in teaching also means teachers must have adequate supplies and support to do their work.

- Today, only about 1 percent of the public school budget is used for textbooks, teaching equipment, and supplies.

- And a survey of 450 science teachers revealed that—in 1981—60 percent of the schools were cutting still further their equipment and supplies budget in laboratory science.

While conducting school visits for the Carnegie high school report, we met one science teacher at a large urban high school who talked of his despair. He said: "When I entered through the door of this classroom for the first time, I was as depressed as I was when getting on the plane to Vietnam. The doors on the cupboards and workbenches were torn off. The equipment was broken, and when I went to the back storage room for the chemicals it was even more depressing . . . I have little money for equipment, no accelerator timer, the pulleys are broken, there are few experiments where all the necessary equipment works."

This picture is perhaps too gloomy. More typical may be the story of Ben Eichelberger who—in a middle income district—left science teaching because of a feeling of being trapped. He said: "I have five classes and four different preparations. During one week I have to collect tickets at the basketball game. I had to beg for everything—even equipment for experiments—because I didn't have a budget." Ben Eichelberger will earn about $30,000 this year as an electrician.

We conclude that school boards—and the community at large—should understand that schools must have adequate budgets to provide students and teachers the tools they need to do the job. Here again, higher education has a role to play.

· Colleges can make laboratory equipment available—on loan—to a science teacher in the schools.

· College labs can be used occasionally by high school students and their teachers.

· College science professors can collaborate with school science teachers to complete an inventory of what the school lab requires.

· And college officials can testify before school boards to urge more adequate support.

Incidentally, just this week I received a call from an executive at Monsanto who described a program of bringing their own scientists as special lecturers into selected public schools in St. Louis. He also spoke of the prospect of making available surplus, but up-to-date, lab equipment needed by the schools. Exploring possibilities such as this may be precisely what colleges and schools in a given region can do together.

Further, to achieve excellence in teaching, schools and colleges should work together to provide, for teachers, more recognitions and rewards. While it will not be possible fully to close the gap between teaching salaries and salaries in the corporate world, ways must be found to improve the tangible and intangible benefits of teaching.

Today, it is especially disturbing that *good* teachers are not financially rewarded for their work. The notion seems to be that if you're good you will move out of teaching and become a counselor or administrator—or a football coach. Good teachers must be recognized and moved forward *within* the profession, not outside it. Consider the possibility of having special ranks—senior teacher or master teacher—to reward good instructors and help beginning teachers, too.

Again, colleges and the corporate world have an important role to play. In the future, some school faculty may have joint appointments with industry and business or with a higher learning institution. And, on another level, special recognitions can be given.

· Princeton University, for example, honors, every year, the five outstanding teachers in New Jersey.

· At Georgetown, and at other higher learning institutions, an honorary degree is awarded to an outstanding teacher in the schools.

· Some colleges cite alumni who have had a distinguished career in teaching.

Clearly, every college and university in the nation should, in some fashion, systematically recognize excellence in teaching in the nation's public schools.

Finally, secondary and higher education should work together to promote the *continued* schooling of the teachers. A 1981 survey revealed that 79 percent of the science teachers had not completed a ten hour course or workshop in the last ten years. And 40 percent reported never having attended an inservice course or workshop since they began teaching—an average of fifteen years!

In contrast, Japan, in 1960, set up special Science Education Centers in all of the nation's 46 prefecturs—offering tuition-free programs to teachers to learn about the latest developments in science. These centers have since broadened to include all school subjects and, ironically, much of the teaching material used is imported from the United States.

In President Reagan's 1984 budget there is—in addition to the $50 million scholarship program—a $19 million program to enrich math and science teaching. The focus of this program is appropriate—but, frankly, the ground rules are disturbing. The proposed grants are to be given, not to schools, but to higher learning institutions. Why is it that whenever we want to improve teaching in the *school*, we give the money to professors in the *college?* I believe the proposed grants in this federal initiative should support *joint* school–college projects. Principals and teachers should be given the opportunity to help shape continuing education programs, rather than wait for colleges—unilaterally—to decide what schools do and do not need.

Incidentally, in the 1984 education budget—which it now appears Congress will expand—the administration is also asking for one million dollars for awards to outstanding teachers in science and mathematics. This program, while relatively small, may, in the long run, be the most significant of all. When we begin to honor excellence in the classroom then, I believe, the effective recruitment of good teachers can begin again.

And now I return to the point where I began. Collaboration between colleges and schools is an important and growing movement in the nation. Clearly, such a partnership will advance excellence in teaching and help relieve the current crisis in science and mathematics.

But the potential for such cooperation can be no greater than our ability to agree on common goals. Efforts to improve cooperation will be unproductive so long as the objectives of the eight years of high school and college remain unclear. Experiments will come and go. Projects will die. New ones will be born. But no sense of continuity will emerge.

Collaboration is, after all, a means to a larger, more essential end. Partnerships will take root only as schools and colleges have a shared vision and a common understanding as to where they should be going.

I am convinced that as schools and colleges work together:

- to strengthen early education;

- define the academic core;

- promote the gifted;

- recruit, for teaching, outstanding students, and

- give teachers adequate tools and appropriate recognition,

then, the theme of this conference—excellence in teaching—becomes an achievable objective.

For those who make the effort, the rewards are high and students are well served.

There can be no better reason for colleges and schools to work together.

Making the Connections

Association for Supervision and Curriculum Development
Washington, DC
March 27, 1993

I'M DELIGHTED TO JOIN YOU at this convocation which celebrates the 50th Anniversary of the Association of Supervision and Curriculum Development. ASCD is one of the nation's most distinguished and effective educational associations. You have, throughout the years, focused on teaching and on learning. The goal of this association has always been to achieve excellence for all, and for fifty years you have been a true community of learning. I salute all of you assembled in this room for your dedicated and inspired service to the nation and, most especially, to children.

This morning I would like to talk about a question that has perplexed educators and philosophers and parents for centuries. What is an educated person? And then, more precisely, I should like to address the question, What should we be teaching students in our schools as we approach the twenty-first century? To put my remarks in a larger context, I'll begin by telling you a story.

In 1972, I was sitting at my desk in Albany, New York. It was a dreary Monday morning and to avoid the pressures of the day I turned instinctively to the stack of third-class mail that I kept perched precariously on the corner of my desk to create the illusion of being very, very busy—it's an old administrative trick. On the top of the heap was the student newspaper from Stanford University. One headline announced that the faculty there had reintroduced a required course in "Western Civilization," after having abolished this requirement just three years before. Bear in mind, it was 1972. The students, I discovered, were mightily offended by the faculty's brash act. In a front-page editorial, they declared that "a required course is an illiberal act." Then the editors concluded with this question: "How dare they impose uniform standards on nonuniform people?"

At first I was amused, and then deeply troubled. I was troubled that, after fourteen or more years of formal learning, some of America's most gifted students still had not learned the simple truth that even though we, as a people, are "nonuniform," we still have many things in common. They had not learned the essential fact that, with all of our diversity, we have characteristics at the core of our existence that bind us to each other.

This brings me to the central theme of my remarks this morning. Being an educated person surely means becoming well informed. It means developing one's own aptitudes and interests, and discovering the diversity that makes us each unique. But there is another side to the equation, and it's called *connections*.

Today, almost all students in the nation's schools complete their Carnegie units, and they are handed a diploma. But in our fragmented academic world, what they fail to gain is a more coherent view of knowledge, and a more integrated, more authentic view of life. Learning for far too many students has become an exercise in trivial pursuit. And for far too long, education in this country has been based on seat time, not on learning.

I'm convinced the time has come to bury the old Carnegie unit. And since the Foundation I now head created this unit of academic measure nearly a century ago, I feel authorized this morning officially to declare it obsolete. I also am convinced that the proposed National Assessment program should not be implemented until we are very clear about what schools should be teaching as we enter the next century.

But what should we be teaching our students? Just what does it mean to be an educated person? An educated person is well informed and continues learning. But to be truly educated means going beyond the isolated facts, putting learning in larger context, and, above all, it means discovering the connectedness of things.

Of course, students should become knowledgeable in history, literature, science, and the rest. But what we urgently need today are students who can see relationships and patterns and put their learning in perspective. For this to be accomplished we need a more thematic curriculum, one that goes beyond the separate academic subjects and uses the disciplines to illuminate larger, more integrative ends. But where do we begin?

Several years ago, in a book called *A Quest for Common Learning*, I suggested that we organize the school curriculum not on the basis of disciplines or departments, but on the basis of what might be called "the core commonalities." By core commonalities, I mean those universal experiences that are shared by all people and all cultures on the planet and make us truly human. While reflecting on the possibility of this basic thematic structure, I concluded that there are, in fact, eight commonalities that bind us to each other.

THE LIFE CYCLE

At the most basic level, we all share the universal human experience of birth, and growth, and death. The life cycle binds us all together. Yet the sad truth is that most students go through life without reflecting on the mystery of their own existence. They complete twelve or even sixteen years of formal schooling not considering the sacredness of their own bodies, not learning how to sustain wellness, and not pondering the imperative of death.

It's really shocking that young people in America today grow up knowing more about their Walkmans or the carburetor of a car than they do about the characteristics of their own bodies. With such ignorance it's easy for young people to do great violence to their bodies. Far too many become addicted to alcohol and drugs. And we are raising a generation of children who have shockingly poor nutrition.

If I were reshaping the school curriculum to help students see connections, I would have, at the very core of common learning, one major strand of study called the "Life Cycle." The focus would be on nutrition, health, and wellness. Every student, for an applied project, would care for some form of life.

Being truly educated means learning about how one's own body functions. It means observing a variety of life forms. And, above all, it means reflecting sensitively on the mystery of birth and growth and death.

LANGUAGE

In addition to the life cycle, all people on the planet use symbols to express feelings and ideas. After our first breath, we start making sounds as a way of reaching out to others. We start developing language in order to connect. A quality education surely means becoming proficient in the written and the spoken word, and discovering that math is a symbol system, too. Our sophisticated use of language sets human beings apart from all other forms of life. Through the miracle of words and other symbols, we are all connected to each other.

Consider the miracle of this very moment. I stand here vibrating my vocal cords. Molecules are bombarded in your direction. They hit your tympanic membrane; signals go scurrying up your eighth cranial nerve, and there's a response deep in your cerebrum that approximates, I trust, the images in mine. But do you realize the audacity of this act?

Language is not just another subject. It's the means by which all other subjects are pursued. The new curriculum, then, should contain a second strand called "The Use of Symbols," which might include the history of language, a study of literature, and a study of mathematics as a symbol system. And surely it also would include speaking and listening, reading and writing across the whole curriculum, since it's through clear writing that clear thinking can be taught.

Above all, students should be asked to consider the ethics of communication, since good language means not just *accuracy* but *honesty* as well. Today, students live in a world where obscenities abound. They live in a world where politicians use sixty-second sound bites to destroy the integrity of their opponents. They live in a world where clichés have become substitutes for reason. Students in the nation's schools urgently need to be taught how to distinguish between communication that is deceitful and communication that is authentic.

To be an educated person means writing with clarity, reading with comprehension, being able to effectively speak, and listen, and accurately compute. Beyond all this, education for the next century also means helping students understand that language is a sacred trust and that truth is the obligation we assume when we are empowered in the use of words.

THE ARTS

Beyond the life cycle and beyond the use of symbols, all people on the planet respond to the aesthetic. Dance is a universal language. Architecture is a universal language. Music is a universal language. Painting and sculpture are languages that can be understood all around the world. Isn't it amazing how Salvador Dali's painting called *The Persistence of Memory* can profoundly communicate to any person haunted by the relentless passage of time? Isn't it remarkable how the gospel song "Amazing Grace" can stir a common bond among people whether they are from Appalachia or Manhattan? Isn't it inspiring how "We Shall Overcome," when sung in slow and solemn cadence, can stir powerful feelings regardless of race or economic status? Archeologists, when they study past civilizations, examine the artifacts of art—the pottery, cave paintings, and musical instruments—to determine the quality of a culture.

The arts are, above all, the special language of children, who even before they learn to speak, respond intuitively to dance, music, and color. And the arts are uniquely helpful to children who are disabled. Every student who enrolls in school has the innate urge and capacity to be artistically expressive. And it's really tragic that for many children the universal language of the arts is suppressed, and then destroyed, in the early years of learning, because school boards consider art a frill.

For the most intimate, most profound, and most moving experiences in our lives, we turn to music and dance and to the visual arts to express feelings and ideas words cannot convey. To be a truly educated person, then, surely means being sensitively responsive to the universal language of art, which should be a central strand of the curriculum in every school.

TIME AND SPACE

This brings me to the fourth "human commonality." While we are all nonuniform, and while we differ dramatically from each other, the simple truth is that all people on the planet have the marvelous capacity to place themselves in time and space. We explore our sense of space through geography and astronomy. We explore our sense of time through the study of history. And yet, how often we squander this truly awesome capacity to look in both directions, even neglecting our personal roots.

Looking back, the most important mentor in my own life was my Grandpa Boyer—who incidentally lived to be one hundred. Grandpa, at the age of forty, moved his little family into the slums of Dayton, Ohio. He then spent the next forty years running a city mission, working for the poor, teaching me more by deed than word that to be truly human one must serve. And yet, for far too many children the influence of such intergenerational models has diminished or totally disappeared.

Margaret Mead said on one occasion that the health of any culture is sustained when three generations are vitally interacting with each other—a "vertical culture" in which the different age groups are connected. And yet in America today we're creating a "horizontal culture," with each generation living all alone. Infants are in nurseries, toddlers are in day care, older children are in schools organized by age. College students are isolated on campuses. Adults are in the workplace. And older citizens are in retirement villages, living and dying all alone.

For several years, my own parents chose to live in a retirement village where the average age was eighty. But this village had a day care center there, too, and all the three- and four-year olds met with their adopted grandparents every day. When I called my father, he didn't talk about his aches and pains. He talked about his little friend. And when I visited, I saw that, like any proud grandparent, my father would have the child's drawings taped to the wall. As I watched them together, I was struck that there is something really moving about a four-year-old seeing the difficulty and courage of growing old. And I was struck, too, by watching an eighty-year-old being informed and inspired by the energy and innocence of a child.

I'm convinced the time has come to build intergenerational institutions that bring the old and young together. I'm impressed by the "grandteacher" programs in the schools, for example, and in the new core curriculum, with a strand called "Time and Space," students should discover their own roots, and complete perhaps an oral history.

But beyond their own extended family, all students should become well informed about the influence of the culture that surrounds them and learn about the traditions of other cultures, too. To put it simply, students should study *western* civilization to understand our past, and they should study *non-western* cultures to understand our future.

In a larger sense, a truly educated person is one who sees connections by placing his or her life in time and space.

GROUPS AND INSTITUTIONS

In addition to the life cycle, the use of symbols, and our shared sense of time, all people on the planet hold membership in groups and institutions that consequentially shape their lives. To be truly educated, means learning about the social web of our existence. It means affirming family life, understanding how governments function, and learning about the informal social structures that surround us. And it also means discovering how group life varies from one culture to another.

Our son Craig lives in a Mayan village in the jungle of Belize with his Mayan wife and four children. When my wife, Kay, and I visit Craig each year, I'm impressed that Mayans and Americans carry on their work in very similar ways. The jungle of Manhattan and the jungle of Belize are separated by a thousand miles and a thousand years, and yet the Mayans, just like us, have their family units. They have elected leaders and village councils; law enforcement officers and jails, and schools and places they worship. At one level it's all very different, but at another level it's very much the same. Students should not only be introduced to the web of institutions in their own lives, but also engage in cross-cultural studies which would compare, for example, Santa Cruz, California with Santa Cruz, Belize.

We all hold membership in groups and institutions—a fifth strand in the new curriculum.

WORK

This brings me to another commonality we all share. The simple truth is that with all our differences, all people on the planet spend time producing and consuming. A quality education surely means helping students understand and prepare adequately for the world of work. Today young people grow up in a culture preoccupied with *consuming*, with little understanding of what it means to actually *produce*. Students may see their parents bring paper home at night and carry more paper off in the morning, but what is it exactly that parents do?

When I was Chancellor of the State University of New York, I took our youngest son, who was eight, to our cabin in the Berkshires on a weekend. My goal was to build a dock. All day, instead of playing, my son sat at the water's edge, watching me, and that evening, as we drove home, Stephen was quite pensive. Finally, after several miles, he said, "Daddy, I wish you'd grown up to be a carpenter—instead of you-know-what!"

A new, integrative curriculum for the schools should also include a strand called "Producing and Consuming," with each student studying simple economics and different monetary systems, learning how work varies from one culture to another, and completing a work project to gain a respect for craftsmanship.

Several years ago when Kay and I were in China, we were told about a student who had defaced the surface of his desk. As punishment he spent three days in the factory where the desks were made, helping the woodworkers, observing the painstaking effort that was involved. And we were told that, not surprisingly, the student never defaced a desk again. I'm suggesting that the new curriculum might include a strand of producing, consuming, and conserving, preparing students not just for college but also for the world of work.

NATURAL WORLD

This brings us to the seventh core commonality. It's true that all people are different. But it's also true that we are all connected to the ecology of planet Earth, in which, as Lewis Thomas put it, we are embedded as working parts. And to be truly educated for the next century means understanding our connectedness to nature.

David, my four-year-old grandson in Belize, understands these connections very well as he chases birds, bathes in the river, and watches corn being picked, pounded into tortillas, and heated over an open fire. But David's cousins, who live in Boston and Princeton with appliances and asphalt roadways and precooked food, find it enormously more difficult to discover their connectedness to nature.

When I was United States Commissioner of Education, Joan Cooney, the brilliant creator of *Sesame Street*, came to see me one day. She said they wanted to start a new program at Children's Television Workshop on science and technology for junior high school kids, so young people could learn a little more about their world and what they must understand to live. The program subsequently was funded and called "3-2-1 Contact." In doing background work for that project, the creators surveyed some junior high school kids in New York City and asked such questions as: "Where does water come from?" A disturbing percentage answered, "The faucet." And they asked, "Where does light come from?" Students said, "The switch." And they asked, "Where does garbage go?" "Down the chute." These students' sense of connectedness went about as far as the VCR, the refrigerator door, and the light switch in the hall.

I'm suggesting that with all our differences, every single one of us is inextricably connected to the natural world. And all students during their days of formal learning should explore this commonality by studying the principles of science, by discovering how technology profoundly shapes their lives, and, above all, by learning that our very survival on this planet means respecting and preserving the Earth home we share together.

SEARCH FOR MEANING

Finally, all people on the planet, regardless of their unique heritage or tradition, are searching for a larger purpose. We all seek to give special meaning to our lives.

Reinhold Niebuhr put it most precisely when he said, "Man cannot be whole unless he be committed, he cannot find himself, unless he finds a purpose beyond himself." And, when all is said and done, to be truly educated means examining one's own values and beliefs. To state it in the old-fashioned way, it means developing convictions.

During our study of the American high school, I became convinced that we have not just a school problem but a youth problem in this country. I was struck that far too many teenagers feel unwanted, unneeded, and

unconnected to the larger world. Without guidance and direction they lose
their sense of purpose at a very early age.

Vachel Lindsay wrote:

> It is the world's one crime
> its babes grow dull,
>
> . . . .
>
> Not that they sow,
> but that they seldom reap,
> Not that they serve,
> but have no gods to serve,
> Not that they die
> but that they die like sheep.

The tragedy is not death. The tragedy is to die with commitments
undefined, convictions undeclared, and service unfulfilled. And with all the
controversy that surrounds it, a school must be a place where values are
examined, not by dictating answers, but by making honorable the quest.

The search for meaning can be taught most effectively perhaps by great
teachers who model values in their lives. Several years ago, I couldn't sleep
one night, and instead of counting sheep I counted all the teachers that I've
had. Three or four teachers changed my life. What made them truly great?
They were well informed. They could relate their knowledge to students.
They created an active, not passive, climate for learning. And they were open
and authentic human beings—they not only taught their subjects, they
taught themselves.

Values can also be taught through service. And I'm convinced that all
students should complete a community service project, working in day care
centers, retirement villages, or tutoring other kids at school.

What then does it mean to be an educated person? It means respecting
the miracle of life, being empowered in the use of language, and responding
sensitively to the aesthetic. Being truly educated means putting learning in
historical perspective, understanding groups and institutions, having
reverence for the natural world, and affirming the dignity of work. And

above all being an educated person means being guided by values and beliefs and connecting the lessons of the classroom to the realities of life. These are the core competencies that I believe replace the old Carnegie units.

And all of this can be accomplished as schools focus not on seat time, but on students in classrooms that are true communities of learning. I know how idealistic it may sound, but it is my urgent hope that in the century ahead students in the nation's schools will be judged not by their performance on a single test but by the quality of their lives. It's my hope that students in the classrooms of tomorrow will be encouraged to be creative, not conforming, learning to cooperate rather than compete. It is my driving hope that students in our schools will begin to see the world as whole and be inspired both by the beauty as well as the challenges of the world around them.

Above all, it is my urgent prayer that Julie, my four-year-old granddaughter who lives in Princeton, and David, her four-year-old cousin in Belize, along with all other children on this planet, will grow up knowing deep down inside that they are truly members of the same human family, the family to which we are all inextricably connected.

Teaching About Religion in Public Schools

The American Academy of Religion
Kansas City, Missouri
November 24, 1991

WHEN THE AMERICAN SOCIOLOGIST DANIEL BELL was asked to give the Hobhouse Memorial Lecture at the London School of Economics in 1977, he chose as his title, "The Return of the Sacred?" Significantly, he placed a question mark at the end of that provocative title. In this lecture, Bell discussed what he saw as a dramatic resurgence of religious belief in modern culture, and he quoted the great German sociologist Max Weber, who wrote at the end of the nineteenth century, "With the progress of science and technology, man has stopped believing in magic powers, in spirits and in demons. He's lost his sense of prophecy, and above all, he's lost his sense of the sacred." "Reality," Weber wrote, "has become dreary, flat, and utilitarian, leaving a great void in the souls of men which they seek to fill with frivolous activity."

But, as Bell went on to note, "the inexorable progress of science and technology shifted sharply in the twentieth century. Man's reason did not prevent the Holocaust or the mushroom-shaped cloud, and the flatness and dreariness of a wholly utilitarian and secularized society of which Max Weber wrote has taken its toll on the human spirit."

Today we are rediscovering that the sense of the sacred is inextricably interwoven with the most basic of human impulses, the most primal human experiences of birth and growth and death. George Steiner, in reflecting on the Holocaust, captured this spirit when he wrote: "We now know that a man can read Goethe or Rilke in the evening, that he can play Bach and Schubert, and go to his day's work at Auschwitz in the morning." "What grows up inside literate civilization," Steiner asks, "that prepares it for barbarism? What grows up, of course, is knowledge without wisdom, competence without conscience, and viewed more neutrally, learning without perspective."

I've been asked to talk about the role of religion in public education. Before exploring that intriguing subject, I should like to pause for just a moment to celebrate the legal safeguards that have kept the nation's classrooms relatively free of religious indoctrination or coercion, at least in recent years. Throughout history, almost every religious group has at one time or another been persecuted because it deviated from accepted norms, which, of course, are relative and keep changing. And surely we should resist any proposal, no matter how well intended, that would violate the conscience of any individual, no matter how much it appears to violate convention.

When I was a boy growing up in Dayton, Ohio, my parents, as a matter of conscience, did not approve of vaccinations. They believed that faith in God was all that was needed to keep me healthy. But because the school required proof that I had been vaccinated against all of the contagious diseases, I had to get a doctor's certificate granting me an exception. I was, incidentally, the only boy in school who needed such accommodations, a very definite minority. The exception was granted, and even though I've been vaccinated now for many years, I still respect profoundly that acknowledgment of conscience. I also grew up in a peace church and my parents objected conscientiously to war. During the war, we had bond drives in the school, and I would keep my class from winning prizes month after month because I didn't buy the stamps.

Looking back, my conflicts were relatively minor in the larger context of religious persecution, although at the time they didn't seem so minor. I felt the sting of students and even some teachers who ridiculed my acts of conscience and insisted that I conform. Through these encounters, I experienced firsthand the conflict between personal conscience and institutionally imposed social norms. The good news is that I was not forced to violate my conscience, even though the social pressure was intense, and these little exercises became absolutely seminal in my judgments about the imposition of religious expectations.

I accept it as a cardinal principle that no involuntary religious act or ceremonial engagement should be imposed on any student in the school. That includes prayer, whether spoken or in silence, since, as a Quaker, silence has a powerful religious significance to me. When the school prayer issue was being debated in the New Jersey legislature, I was appalled that silence was being pushed as an alternative, with the argument that it was just a moment of "doing nothing." Silence that is intended to have a spiritual consequence is not a moment of doing nothing. It's a moment of doing something profoundly religious, and we cannot skirt the issue by suggesting that the processes of prayer only include the utterances of words. Simply stated, no public school should teach religion or impose religious ritual on its students. These are obligations that should be entrusted to the church and, above all, to parents.

This brings me to the central theme of my remarks today. While no school should impose religious belief or practice, I believe that it's simply impossible to be a well educated person without exploring how religion has shaped the human story in almost every culture throughout history. And I believe that the sacred texts of all the great religions should be introduced to students with reverence and intellectual insight.

Students simply cannot know art without reflecting on the influences of religion, from the Hindu cave paintings, Buddhist art, and temples of Ancient Greece, to Michelangelo and the great cathedrals of the Middle Ages that so inspired Henry Adams and Marc Chagall. They cannot know literature without understanding how religion has shaped the world's great writers, from Homer and Euripedes to T. S. Eliot, John Updike, and I. B. Singer. Students cannot know music without grasping the power of religion in inspiring performers and composers from Hildegard, the great twelfth century nun/composer, to Leonard Bernstein.

Virtually every discipline has been influenced by religion. In psychology we have William James' landmark study, *The Varieties of Religious Experience*, and in sociology we have Max Weber's classic work, *The Protestant Ethic and the Spirit of Capitalism*. And, of course, there's no conceivable way for students to understand the conflicts in the Middle East or Northern Ireland, or our own history here in the United States, without understanding the consequential role of religion.

A few years ago, I chaired a commission of the Williamsburg Charter to advise in the preparation of a curriculum guide for the study of First Amendment rights. That guide explored the growth of religion, religious conflicts in this country, great clergymen in our past, the conflicts over school prayer, and all the rest, based on the premise that students cannot know the United States without an understanding of religion. I'm suggesting that it's simply unimaginable to have quality education in the nation's schools without including in the course of study a consideration of how religion has been a central thread in the very fabric of the human story, both here and all around the world.

Ten years ago, when the United States Department of Education surveyed the study of religion in public schools, only 640 of the 15,000 high schools in this country offered even one course labeled "religion" or "comparative religion," and only two percent of the public school students were so enrolled. There's no evidence that the situation has altered in recent years. Not only do we not have courses that are clearly and explicitly defined as an inquiry into religion and human culture, even more disturbing, there isn't evidence that other courses are addressing the interrelationship between their subject matter and religion, whether in history, or art, or music, or psychology, or sociology. In these subject areas, religion is rarely introduced. Further, my informal observations tell me that textbooks are virtually silent, or, at least superficial, on the subject, perhaps fearing a backlash that would threaten sales.

It's my hope, then, that while the current school reform movement endeavors to strengthen math and science teaching to make us "world-class," we also can begin to acknowledge more openly that the study of religion is an essential dimension of excellence as well. I happen to agree with Justice Arthur Goldberg who, when he wrote his opinion on the school prayer decision in 1963, made the following observation: "Neither government nor this Court can or should ignore the fact that a vast portion of our people believe in and worship God and that many of our legal, political, and personal values derive historically from religious teachings." Justice Goldberg concluded, "It seems clear to me that the Court would recognize the propriety of teaching *about* religion, as distinguished from the teaching *of* religion, in the public schools." As they say in Washington, "I therefore rest my case."

This brings me to yet another compelling issue. Is there any way to introduce in the schools not just a study about religion, but what Daniel Bell called "the sense of the sacred?" Can the schools help students put their learning in larger historical, social, and ethical perspective? I am less interested, frankly, in revising teaching in the disciplines than in addressing the attitudes of students toward this essential but ephemeral idea of "the sense of the sacred." I am convinced that in addition to learning about religion during their course of formal study, students should be asked to explore moral and ethical issues of great consequence; to gain perspective by putting their academic work in larger context; and, one might also hope, to develop an ethical framework of their own, which may be a derivative of religion. Let me quickly offer four examples to illustrate this larger point.

First, it is my conviction that we can teach values in the schools—or, if you will, a "sense of the sacred"—by giving priority to language. Malcolm Bradbury writing in the *New York Times*, said, "It's an old truth that if we do not have mastery over our language, language itself will master us. We discover life," he said, "through language." Language is the most essential, the most awesomely important human function. It starts in the womb, as the unborn infant monitors the mother's voice. And I think it no accident that the three middle ear bones—the hammer, the anvil, and the stirrup— are the only bones that are fully formed at birth. We start by listening, and then we learn to talk, first through gurgles and coos and eventually through full sentences. As a requirement for life, for survival, we reach out to others from the earliest days of our lives through the miraculous symbol system we call language.

We might even pause and reflect on the miracle of this moment, which we so casually take for granted. I come to the platform. I start vibrating my vocal cords and molecules go bombarding in your direction. They hit your tympanic membrane and signals go scurrying up your eighth cranial nerve, and there's a response deep in your cerebrum which, I trust, approximates the images in mine. But consider the audacity of this act. It is an unbelievable act of faith! The ability to be intellectually and evocatively connected is a wonderful and awesome function that we use every day of our lives. And yet students can go from birth to death and are not asked to reflect carefully on this God-given, gene-driven capacity.

Language sustains the human culture. Without it, there are no connections. With it, we can bond intellectually and evocatively and move the human story forward. And yet students today are living in a world where language is debased, where obscenities abound. They live in a world where politicians use sixty-second sound bites to destroy the integrity of opponents, and where language is used to conceal much more than it reveals. My sadness about the recent Supreme Court hearings had less to do with the personal charges being hurled than with my feeling that somehow language was being used to evade the truth, not to expose integrity at its best.

Thus I'm convinced that teaching language in the schools must emphasize not just skill at sending the message, but sensitivity in listening as well. Wayne Booth, at the University of Chicago, wrote on one occasion, that our efforts to speak and listen are often a vicious cycle moving downward. But he went on to say, "We've all experienced moments when the spiral moved upward, when one party's effort to speak and listen just a little bit better produced a similar response, making it possible," he said, "to move on up the spiral to moments of genuine understanding."

In essence, I'm suggesting that the teaching of language is teaching about *truth*, and that every language class must be an ethics class, since communication without honesty is one of life's most dangerous and destructive weapons. At present, we seem to be concerned about syntax and structure, but rarely do we infuse the minds of students with the fact that language must be bathed in honesty and integrity or else we have made fraudulent one of humanity's most essential functions. Every class should be concerned about the quality of language and every school should introduce a course in the ethics of communication to help students analyze propaganda, and understand that messages must be measured, not just by the correctness of their structure, but by the integrity of their content, too.

T. Elton Trueblood, long-time president of Earlham College, wrote recently about one of his mentors at Johns Hopkins. Dr. Trueblood said that he had to write a paper every week and the professor would make marginal notes about the syntax and the grammar; but always at the bottom of the paper, underlined, were these words: "But is it true? Is it really true?!" I'm suggesting that strengthening values in education means teaching students that language is a sacred trust and that honesty is the obligation we assume when we're empowered with the use of words.

This leads me to suggestion number two. In addition to teaching about the great influence that religion has had in the history of the human story, and the sacredness of language, let's also look at the coherence of the curriculum. I believe we urgently need to shape a curriculum that shows relationships, not fragmentation. Today's students are offered a grab-bag of isolated courses. They complete the required credits, but what they fail to gain is a more coherent view of knowledge and a more integrated, more authentic view of life. To put it simply, their sense of the sacred is diminished.

During the 1960s, I met frequently with students who said that we had nothing in common, because I was over thirty and because I was running a corrupt university. I was fascinated that they kept insisting we had nothing in common. And I was troubled that we have educated students to understand individualism but have not reminded them of their essential connections. We affirm differences, but fail to capture the commonalities. And in the absence of larger loyalties, we're settling for little loyalties. Students are hunkering down in their separate interests failing to find the relationships that bind.

This led me to try to identify the human commonalities that might be an organizing framework for a larger, more integrative course of study. I finally concluded that there are eight universal experiences that bind us all together—all cultures, all people on the planet—and these might be the means by which our students could discover the fabric of integration.

First, we are all bound together by the imperative of birth and growth and death, and at the core of every curriculum should be a study of the life cycle—the miracle of our own existence, the majesty of conception, the inevitability of death. Second, we are all connected through our ability to use symbols, as I've discussed. Third, every human being on the planet responds to the aesthetic. Fourth, we are all members of groups and institutions, even though they differ from one culture to another. Fifth, there is a natural world, "an enormous imponderable system of life in which we're embedded," as Lewis Thomas said, "as working parts." To understand ecology and our place in it is absolutely crucial. Sixth, we all can recall the past and anticipate the future, a marvelous capacity that we do not exercise well these days. Seventh, we all engage in producing and consuming, though far too many people in this country are preoccupied with consumption and have very little understanding of production. Finally, we all search for ultimate meaning and purpose in our lives. And it's here that religion plays a central role in our intellectual quest.

Mark Van Doren said over fifty years ago that "the connectedness of things is what the educator contemplates to the limit of his capacity. . . . The student who can begin early in his life to think of things as connected . . . has begun the life of learning." This, it seems to me, is what the sense of the sacred is all about—discovering ultimate relationships and patterns. Stephen Hawking, in his brilliant book *A Brief History of Time*, suggests that if we discover the ultimate and unifying theme of the universe we will, finally, discover the mind of God.

This leads me to suggestion number three. Students can discover the sense of the sacred through the symbol system we call language, and they can begin to see relationships and patterns through a core of common learning. But in the end, it is the teacher in the classroom who embodies the value system and relates knowledge to human values.

All of us have been influenced by an outstanding teacher. What is it that makes these teachers great? Every great teacher has four characteristics: first, they know their subject; second, they know their students; third, there is active participation, and finally—and this is to the point of my remarks this morning—they are honest and authentic human beings, that is, there is an integrity in what they say and how they live that gives power to their message. I absolutely believe that the value system of a school or college is sustained, in the end, not through the curriculum, but through the integrity of great teachers. And this leads me to my final observation.

I think that schools can help students develop a sense of the sacred by engaging them in service, by helping them see some relationship between what they learn and how they live. During our study of the American high school several years ago, I became convinced that we have not just a school problem, but also a youth problem in this country. When I went into high schools, I was impressed at the sense of anonymity that overwhelmed most of those institutions. Most of the students were not known by adults. Only the very good and the very bad had caught the attention of the managers of the system. The vast majority walked from class to class anonymously, unknown as human beings. I concluded that many dropped out because no one had noticed that they had, in fact, dropped in.

If we want to make one change in the schools that would make a difference and cut the number of dropouts, it would be to somehow understand the dignity of every single student, and to make sure that each one is known and connected to the adult world. One way to accomplish this is to break up large schools into smaller units of no more than five hundred students each, and to assign every student to a group of no more than twenty. Each group would meet with a mentor at the beginning of each day, not someone who would just take attendance, but someone who would discover who these students are and recognize their dignity.

I also would like to see every student complete a community service term, to become engaged in retirement villages or in day-care centers, in youth camps or even in tutoring other kids at school. Everyone knows that the best way to learn is to teach, and yet we do not encourage students to interact with others or to help the younger generation. I am especially intrigued at the idea of having students engaged in retirement villages with older people. The intergenerational isolation in this country is a profoundly important social ill. Margaret Mead said on one occasion that "the continuity of all cultures depends on the living presence of at least three generations." And yet we're creating a kind of horizontally layered culture in which the age groups are isolated and go from birth to death never talking to one other. I think grandparents and grandchildren belong together, and I believe it increasingly as I grow older.

Here, then, is my conclusion: it's an absolute imperative, I believe, that public education remain free of sectarian control and that the conscience of every student be vigorously affirmed. At the same time, students should surely study about religion and its influence throughout history. They should understand that the search for meaning is universal and that religion has profoundly shaped the human experience on the planet.

I'm convinced that schools can be more attentive to "the sense of the sacred" through the study of language, which at its best is a study of values; through a curriculum that shows coherence and what I view as divine patterns; through great teaching that nurtures the intellect as well as integrity and human justice, and through a term of service that demonstrates to students that to be truly human, one must serve.

Lifelong Learning in the Arts

National Endowment for the Arts
Chicago, Illinois
April 16, 1994

I AM DELIGHTED TO JOIN YOU at this magnificent celebration. And, on behalf of all of us, I wish to express deep gratitude to Jane Alexander for giving such superb leadership and inspiration to the nation, bringing us all together to affirm lifelong learning in the arts as a seamless web.

This is a moment of new beginnings in America. As a public, we are beginning to recognize that the quality of a culture and the quality of the arts are inextricably interlocked. We're beginning to understand more fully that if we do not educate our children in the symbol system we call art, we will lose not only our civility, but our humanity as well.

No education is complete without the arts and I am enormously encouraged that just three weeks ago the arts were defined, by federal legislation, as a core subject for all the nation's schools. I wish to congratulate Secretary Richard Riley, Senator Edward Kennedy, and all the legislative leaders for affirming the centrality of art in the education of children.

It is my deep conviction that artistic expression is one of humankind's most essential forms of language. In most respects, the human species is far less well equipped than other creatures on the planet. We're no match for the lion in strength; we're outstripped by the ostrich in speed; we can't outswim the dolphin; we see less acutely than the hawk. Yet, as humans, we excel in the exquisite use of symbols—which empowers us to outdistance all other forms of life in what we see, and feel, and know.

There is, in short, one incontrovertible conclusion to be reached. The arts are not a frill. They are deeply embedded in that which makes us truly human.

First, we need the arts to express feelings and ideas that words cannot convey. In the dawn of civilization, our early ancestors used sounds and simple gestures to convey feelings and ideas. Then words were formed, a vocabulary took shape, followed by written symbols, making it possible to send messages from place to place and to transmit knowledge, miraculously, from one generation to another.

But even with all the beauty of the written and spoken word, language was incomplete. There remained, deeply buried in the bosom of the human spirit, experiences that could not be captured by the verbal utterances we call words. Words could *not* portray sufficiently the joy of a spring morning or the fruits of a fall harvest or the grief and loneliness that marked the ending of a love relationship. They could not adequately convey the babbling of the brook or the setting of the evening sun.

The full range of human experiences—physical, emotional, and spiritual—cannot be captured in words alone. For the most intimate, most profoundly moving experiences, we need more subtle symbols. And so it is that men and women have, throughout history, turned to music, dance, and the visual arts.

Several years ago, I read an interview with physicist Victor Weisskopf, who was discussing the Big Bang theory. Near the end of this provocative conversation, Weisskopf said that if you wish to understand the Big Bang theory you should "listen to the works of Haydn." At first I was amused and a bit bewildered by this proposition. Yet, upon reflection, the point was absolutely clear. Weisskopf was reminding us that occasionally human experiences are so profound, so intellectually and evocatively overwhelming, they call for symbols beyond words or numbers for full expression. The Big Bang theory, he was saying, must be *felt* as well as *thought*.

Conductor Murry Sidlin put it this way: "When words are no longer adequate, when our passion is greater than we are able to express in a usual manner, people turn to art. Some people go to the canvas and paint, some stand up and dance. But we all go beyond our normal means of communicating, and this is the common human experience for all people on this planet."

Especially compelling is the way young children, even before they learn to speak, turn instinctively to rhythm and song, and color and visual patterns. And lifelong learning in the arts must begin long before school itself. It's in the first years of life when a child's knowledge exponentially expands. This is the time when curiosity abounds, when children are actively absorbing their surroundings, when they are listening, touching, and seeing the world so they can learn.

Wouldn't it be wonderful if singing and painting and rhythm were woven into the fabric of every family? Wouldn't it be wonderful if every preschool and every day care center were a place of beauty? And wouldn't it be wonderful if every neighborhood had music and dance and theatre for children?

We have in the United States today, 19 million preschoolers who watch television 15 billion hours every year. And wouldn't it be wonderful if we had a "Ready to Learn" cable channel with music and poetry and theatre and painting, a channel dedicated exclusively to art programming for young children? After all, we have channels for news and sports and sex and weather and junk jewelry and kid's cartoons. Is it unthinkable that we would have at least one channel to enrich the aesthetic experiences of children?

I'm convinced that lifelong learning in the arts should begin in the very first years of a child's life, to encourage the full development of his or her potential.

Beyond expressing feelings and insights words cannot convey, the arts are necessary to extend the child's ways of knowing and to bring creativity to the classroom.

When children first come to school, they're filled with questions. In fact, four-year-olds ask, on average, 437 questions every day. Young children keep asking "why," responding to their own curiosity and intuition. But after several years of schooling they typically stop asking "why" and begin to ask, "Will we have this on the test?"

When I was United States Commissioner of Education I heard heated debates over whether art was an *academic discipline* or a *creative act*. I've long believed that the arts serve both objectives. There is, of course, an academic content to be studied, just as there is in every other form of language. Great art, like great literature, bears a legacy to be remembered and studied. It has precise forms to be understood and mastered. And the connections between art and culture must be intellectually examined.

But there is another side to the equation. Harvard psychologist Howard Gardner reminds us that children have not only verbal intelligence, they also have social intelligence, spatial intelligence, intuitive intelligence, and aesthetic intelligence. And in the arts, students learn to think not just in linear fashion, but intuitively and creatively, as well.

Several years ago at a commencement exercise at Mt. Union College in Ohio, the valedictorian speaker said that during spring break she sat down to color with her five-year-old niece. The niece took the crayons and the book and quickly leafed passed the thirty or more line drawings and began to color on the blank page in the back. When asked why she chose to color where there was no picture, the little girl replied firmly: "Outside the lines you can do anything you want."

Walt Whitman, in the opening lines of *Leaves of Grass*, declared, "I celebrate myself." We need art in every school, from kindergarten to grade twelve, to encourage all students to continue to color outside the lines.

The arts extend language. They encourage creativity and give children new ways of knowing. But we also need the arts to help students integrate learning and discover the connectedness of things.

In today's fragmented academic world, students complete the separate academic subjects. They are handed a diploma, but what they fail to gain is a more coherent view of knowledge and a more integrated, more authentic view of life. Albert Einstein wrote that religion, art, and science are branches of the same tree. But where are students invited to discover connections such as these? On most campuses, artists and scientists live in separate worlds.

In the early 1970s, while serving as Chancellor of SUNY, I helped organize the New York State Theatre, which creatively uses drama in schools to promote integrative learning in all the disciplines. And during the past quarter century, literally thousands of other school-based programs have demonstrated, beyond question, that the arts can bring coherence to our fragmented academic world—and improve performance, too. I'm convinced that connections across the disciplines can be accomplished most authentically through the integrative power of the arts.

The arts, while essential for all, have special meaning for children who are socially insecure, emotionally distressed, or physically restricted.

Many years ago, as a young medical audiologist, I worked with children who were deaf. Because they couldn't hear, they couldn't speak, and I saw the frustration and rage children experience when they can't communicate with others. These youngsters were often very gifted, but without the miracle of language they lived in a lonely and isolated world. I also observed that, through the arts, these same children would stand up and dance or put paint to canvas or weave an artistic pattern, and suddenly life for them became more fulfilling and complete.

For the past dozen years I've chaired Very Special Arts, a program of the Kennedy Center that promotes arts for the disabled. I've seen, time and time again, how both children and adults who are physically or linguistically restricted can communicate joyfully through painting or dance or sculpture or weaving.

On one occasion, at a Kennedy Center symposium, Linda Bovee, a gifted actress, was the luncheon speaker. Because of her deafness, Ms. Bovee spoke using the visual language of "signing," and she was accompanied by a translator to help those of us who were linguistically deficient. Near the end of her presentation, Linda quoted Robert Frost's familiar poem: "Two roads diverged in a wood, and I / I took the one less traveled by, / And that has made all the difference." As Ms. Bovee moved her hands and revealed an intensity of feeling on her face, I found the visual signals even more powerful and more elegant than the spoken word.

The language of the arts, without question, has a very special meaning for disabled children, and through music and dance and the visual arts they can become confidently self-expressive.

The arts can be powerfully motivating for young people who are socially alienated, too. During the Carnegie study of the American high school, I became convinced that we have not just a school problem, but a youth problem in this nation. Far too many teenagers in this country feel unneeded, unwanted, and unconnected to the world. Even in the school itself, students drift aimlessly from class to class.

Several years ago I visited a huge inner-city school where the principal said that the students for years had vandalized a large wall next to the playground, covering it with graffiti. One day, he met with student leaders and told them, "The space is yours." Soon the wall was cleared, and a magnificent mural appeared. The wall then remained, he said, respectfully untouched.

It also has been clearly demonstrated that troubled kids who participate in dance and drama and music groups can become, almost overnight, less destructive and more creative.

The arts also can help build community, not only within the school, but beyond the school—in neighborhoods, among different cultures, and across the generations, too.

Lewis Mumford, in *The Myth of the Machine*, reminds us that as societies grew from small villages into impersonal cities, they gained in productivity but lost community. Something similar is happening to us today. And yet, despite the separations, all of us have a deep need for bonding, from the first to the last moments of our lives.

Biologist Mary Clark put it this way: "Social bonds are not temporary contracts entered into for the convenience of an individual. Social embeddedness is," she said, "the essence of our nature." Yet, the sad truth is that, in America today, shared values have begun to fade. We separate ourselves between rich and poor, black and white, young and old.

Many now wonder if it's still possible to discover common ground. I remain convinced that community is not only possible, but essential. I also am convinced that the arts give us the one language that can bridge the chasms that divide. Consider, for example, how Salvador Dali's painting "The Persistence of Memory" speaks to everyone haunted by the passage of time. Consider how Picasso's "Guernica" makes a universal statement about war that can be felt in the heart of every human being. Consider also how the gospel song "Amazing Grace" creates a common bond among people, whether in Appalachia or Manhattan. Consider how "We Shall Overcome," sung in slow and solemn cadence, can bind us all together, regardless of race or age or economic status.

The arts can help build connections by bringing music to the park, festivals to our neighborhoods, and parents to the schools. And the National Endowment's "Design Arts" program supports projects in architecture, landscape, and urban design that enrich the visual environment of communities.

Building community reaches globally as well. In 1974, I traveled with the New York State Children's Theatre to the Soviet Union for a presentation of the *Wizard of Oz* in the Bolshoi Theatre. At the end of the performance, when the American students sang, as encore, "Somewhere Over the Rainbow," in Russian, the Cold War seemed momentarily to melt away.

I know, of course, that artistic messages do not always build bridges of understanding. They also can create confusion, even confrontation. But it is my abiding faith that ultimately the arts will heal. They are, as one first grade teacher put it, "the language of the angels."

A year or so ago I spoke at a commencement in New England. While watching the endless line of graduates, I was buoyed by one senior who had taped on the top of his mortar board this simple message: "Fear No Art." And for the arts to stir trust, not fear, we must celebrate diversity and build cultural institutions in our cities that are, themselves, communities—not enclaves for the privileged.

The arts can build bridges, not only across cultures, but also across the generations—connecting life's beginnings and endings. Yet in America today we are creating a horizontal culture, one in which each age group is separated from the others. We're even institutionalizing the separations. The time has come to build intergenerational institutions, places where grandparents and grandchildren can joyfully communicate through painting, singing, and rhythm.

The arts are, to put it simply, as evocative in the later years as they are in the beginning. Carl Sandburg seemed to be speaking with special meaning about art for the elderly when he wrote:

> Once having marched
> Over the margins of animal necessity,
> Over the grim line of sheer subsistence
> Then man came
> To the deeper rituals of his bones,
> To the lights lighter than any bones,
> To the time for thinking things over,
> To the dance, the song, the story,
> Or the hours given over to dreaming,
> Once having so marched.

In the end, it's through the arts that the life cycle comes full circle.

Here, then, is my conclusion. First, we need the arts to express ideas and feelings in ways beyond words. Second, we need the arts to stir creativity and enrich a child's ways of knowing. Third, we need the arts to integrate the fragments of academic life. Fourth, we need the arts to empower the disabled. And, above all, we need the arts to create community and to build connections across the generations. Learning in the arts truly is a lifelong, deeply satisfying journey.

New Technologies
and the Public Interest

The New York Times
New York, New York
December 13, 1994

WHEN MARTIN SEGAL ASKED ME to join this conversation, I thought immediately about young Robert Benchley who—in a final examination at Harvard College—was asked to discuss the conflict between the Soviet Union and the United States over "off-shore" fishing rights. Hopelessly unprepared, Benchley wrote: "I know nothing about this crisis from the Soviet perspective. I know even less about the U.S. position, so I'd like to discuss the conflict from the viewpoint of the fish, which pretty well sums up my assignment here today."

Specifically, I've been asked to comment briefly on how the intellectual "property rights" debate relates to public interest, to the larger, educational social context. And the answer is, of course, that the two are inextricably interlocked, since nothing in a free society is of greater consequence than how information is gathered and transmitted.

A half century ago, MIT Professor Norbert Weiner observed that society can be understood through a study of the messages and the communication facilities that belong to it. And we are here today precisely because the new "information age" has, during the past fifty years, quite literally transformed the way we live and the way we work and even, perhaps, the way we think.

In the spring of 1946, I made my first trip to New York City with my high school graduating class. And a highlight of that visit was a tour of the NBC Studios where I saw—for the very first time—blurred images on a ten-inch television screen. The guide who led the tour called TV a novelty as I recall it. And my classmates and I agreed that television was—at best—a fascinating gimmick. As coincidence would have it, it was that very same year, 1946, when—just down the road—the nation's first electronic digital computer was unveiled at the University of Pennsylvania. It weighed thirty tons, it filled the space of a two-car garage and it cost half-a-million dollars. A half century has passed and today, 94.2 million American homes—that's 98 percent of all households—have at least one television set.

And today, the nation's 19 million preschoolers watch television 15 billion hours every year. So much for the NBC gimmick! As for computers, the power of that first clumsy model in Philadelphia can now be packaged in a pea-sized silicon chip. And when these two great inventions—computers and televisions—were married in the 1980s, millions of Americans had, for the first time, unprecedented access to new forms of art and education with a quality of transmission virtually indistinguishable from the real.

Today, ordinary citizens, as well as students in our schools, can take field trips electronically to the Smithsonian. They can watch lift-offs at Cape Kennedy, travel to the bottom of the sea, peer inside a human cell, and spend an afternoon at the Louvre in Paris. Students of all ages are now able to browse in the world's great libraries, tour the New York Museum of Natural History, listen to the Philharmonic, watch cheetahs in their natural habitat, be on-line with classmates in Australia. And in such a world, learning—quite literally—has no limits.

But it's also true that for most students, this vision of a global classroom is still largely a potential. The harsh truth is that, while we talk about CD-Roms, most classrooms within minutes of this meeting have only chalkboards, outdated maps, and broken-down projectors. The good news is that, today, an estimated four and a half million computers are installed in the nation's schools; from 1992 to 1993 CD-Rom use increased 93 percent. And nearly 30 percent of the nation's schools are now connected to at least one on-line service.

Still, if all of the technology were suddenly removed from most of the nation's schools, few would hardly notice. Schools may well be the only consequential institution in our culture where that is true. I'm convinced that the first and most compelling challenge we confront in any discussion of technology and the public interest, is to assure that the new technology will close, rather than widen, the gap between the privileged and the disadvantaged. If we fail to achieve in this country both access and excellence for all students, not just the most advantaged, I'm convinced that all of the other information issues will be largely academic.

This leads me to say just a word about intellectual property rights, the subject of this conference. As everyone here knows, the idea of information as property was sewn into our Constitution two centuries ago. It was built deep into our laws, our economy, and our political psyche. It's built into the way we have organized our schools and libraries and museums—pulling together in one place, information that is then cautiously passed on to others.

So long as original works were packaged in books and films and records and paintings, the notion of owning brainwork seemed to hold. But when it became possible to send digital signals, effortlessly and instantaneously, from one hard drive disc to another, information began to slip past the traditional gatekeepers of the culture. An early version of this shift occurred in my own family, about 25 years ago, when our youngest son came home from school and announced, "I learned the alphabet on Sesame Street, but my kindergarten teacher thinks she taught it to me."

Five years ago, former Federal Appeals Judge and our first Secretary of Education, Shirley Hufstedler, observed that, with limited exception, knowledge and even information are, by their very nature, incapable of exclusive possession. And this is especially true in an electronic age when ideas have been reduced to a form that can be read by computers and transmitted by wireless, satellite, or lasers. In such a world, she said, it is increasingly difficult to distinguish the medium from the message or to control either one. Technology is, Hufstedler concluded, moving us toward a global information network that may transform itself into a global information "commons"—where information is owned by everyone, a commons where resources are not depleted, but endlessly renewed.

As an outsider looking in, I have no idea where all of this—legally—will lead, except perhaps to what one lawyer friend of mine approvingly described as "vistas of endless litigation." What *is* clear, however, is that the main thing we must hold onto—and uncompromisingly insist upon—is the need for creativity to be rewarded, so that great writers and great artists are not lost to the public good.

Albert Einstein is often quoted as saying that no problem can be solved from the same conclusions that created it. We must, he said, learn "to see the world as new"—a challenge that seems especially relevant at a time when information has become highly portable, is always leaking, and, I suspect, almost impossible to own.

What I've been discussing thus far is a world Peter Drucker calls "the knowledge society," one in which information is, in fact, our most precious resource. In such a world, education should empower everyone, not the few. But for information to become *knowledge*, and ultimately, one hopes, *wisdom*, it must be organized. And, in this new climate, the *public* interest challenge, beyond access and equity is, I believe, sorting and selection. The challenge of educators is to help students make sense of a world described by some as "information overload."

Recently this matter of overload was put neatly in perspective by my friend Harlan Cleveland, president of the World Academy of Art and Science, who wrote, "When I was growing up I was taught that the key to stuffing my head with useful insights was access to the information I would need. But my very first visit to a great library as a teenage tourist—it happened to be the Library of Congress—cured me of that illusion. Confronting the endless stacks of books," he said, "I quickly figured out that my problem would never be access, but selection." Digital technology, of course, simply exacerbates Harlan's problem.

Consider the Internet, a dazzling gold mine of information which they say is doubling every year. But navigating through this sea of data is becoming more complicated every day. And without highly developed skills, millions of Americans may become intellectually unempowered—and specialists in one field increasingly may lose contact with those in others.

I'm convinced that what our students urgently need today is not just more information, but coherence—the capacity to gain a more coherent view of knowledge and a more integrated, more authentic view of life. There is, then, an urgent need to create a new level of literacy, one that empowers students not only to have access, but to be more selective and more integrative in the information they receive.

This leads to one final observation. Beyond access and beyond selectivity and beyond integration is *credibility*, perhaps the most challenging public interest issue we confront.   Can the messages we receive in the new information age be trusted?

Consider words.   In the world of scholarship where texts can now be endlessly reshuffled, whose works are they anyway?   In music, a technique called "sampling" manipulates snippets from many compositions.   In the visual arts, a recent *Scientific American* story declares that "digital technology has subverted the certainty of photographic evidence."   To prove the point, a cover illustration of the magazine presents Marilyn Monroe and Abraham Lincoln in a cordial arm embrace.   William J. Mitchell concluded this article with this warning: "The information superhighway will bring us a growing flood of information in digital format.   But we will have to take great care to sift the facts from the fictitious and the falsehoods."

When I was growing up in Dayton, Ohio, I'd occasionally hear skeptics say: "Believe half of what you see and nothing that you hear."   Is it possible that we now must tell our children: "Believe nothing that you either see *or* hear."   Isn't it ironic that the very technology that brings us "virtual reality" may also be the source of "non-detectable deception."   In such a world, how can we teach students to be skeptical and discerning, while also urging them to keep faith in our ability to communicate authentically with each other?   Surely, without such trust, civility is lost.

In the summer of 1938, E. B. White said television would become either "a saving radiance in the sky" or an "unbearable disturbance."   And these are precisely the same choices we confront today.   And I'm convinced that whether the new technologies become radiant or disturbing, will, in the end, have far less to do with legalisms, than with *education*.

In the century ahead, we urgently need schools and colleges, museums and galleries, and libraries and newspapers, to go beyond extending access to information and empower students to become more *selective*, more *integrative*, and more *discerning* in their education.   And for this to be accomplished we need, above all else, gifted and inspired teachers.

The simple truth is that almost all of us are here today because of the influence of an inspired teacher.   And in the new information age, public interest is best served, not only by building new electronic highways, but, most especially, by giving new dignity and new status to the sacred act of teaching.

Technology can instantaneously transmit information all around the world. But technology, with all of its dazzling effects, cannot convey wisdom. For this we need educational institutions that help students of all ages become more discerning, teaching the capacity to separate the shoddy from that which is elegant and enduring.

REFERENCES

References

Adler, Mortimer J., *The Paideia Proposal: An Educational Manifesto.* New York: MacMillan, 1982.

Adler, Mortimer, and Charles Van Doren, *How to Read a Book.* New York: Simon and Schuster, 1972.

Agee, James, and Walker Evans, *Let Us Now Praise Famous Men.* New York: Ballantine Books, 1966.

Ashby, Eric, *Technology and the Academics: An Essay on Universities and the Scientific Revolution.* New York: St. Martin's Press, 1966.

Bell, Daniel, *The Winding Passage.* New Brunswick, New Jersey: Transaction Publishers, 1991.

Bellah, Robert, et al., *The Good Society.* New York: Alfred A. Knopf, 1991.

Booth, Wayne, "Mere Rhetoric, Rhetoric, and the Search for Common Learning," in Ernest L. Boyer, *Common Learning.* Washington, DC: The Carnegie Foundation for the Advancement of Teaching, 1981.

Bronowski, Jacob, *Science and Human Values.* New York: Julian Messner, Inc., 1956.

Clark, Mary E., "Meaningful Social Bonding as a Universal Human Need," in *Conflict: Human Needs Theory,* ed. John Burton. New York: St. Martin's Press, 1990.

Cleveland, Harlan, *The Knowledge Executive.* New York: E.P. Dutton, 1985.

Durant, Will, *Our Oriental Heritage,* vol. 1 of *The Story of Civilization.* New York: Simon and Schuster, 1935; copyright renewed, 1963.

Gardner, Howard, *Frames of Mind: The Theory of Multiple Intelligences*. New York: Basic Books, 1983.

Geertz, Clifford, "Blurred Genres: The Refiguration of Social Thought," *The American Scholar*, Spring 1980.

Greenleaf, Robert K., *Servant Leadership: A Journey into the Nature of Legitimate Power and Greatness*. New York: Paulist Press, 1976.

Handlin, Oscar, "Epilogue—Continuities," in Bok, Derek, *Universities and the Future of America*. Durham, North Carolina: Duke University Press, 1990.

Harvard Committee, *General Education in a Free Society*. Cambridge, MA: Harvard University Press, 1945.

Hawking, Stephen W., *A Brief History of Time: From the Big Bang to the Black Hole*. Toronto: Bantam, 1988.

Hochschild, Arlie, *The Second Shift: Working Parents and the Revolution at Home*. New York: Viking, 1989.

Jacoby, Russell, *The Last Intellectuals: American Culture in the Age of Academe*. New York: Basic Books, 1987.

Kerr, Clark, *The Uses of the University, With a "Postscript—1972."* Cambridge, Massachusetts: Harvard University Press, 1972.

King, Martin Luther, *A Testament of Hope: The Essential Writings and Speeches of Martin Luther King, Jr.,* ed. James Melvin Washington. San Francisco: Harper Collins, 1986.

Mead, Margaret, *Culture and Commitment: A Study of the Generation Gap*. Garden City, New York: Natural History Press, 1970.

Mistral, Gabriela, *Llamado por el Nino* (The Call for the Child). 1946.

Niebuhr, Reinhold, *Moral Man and Immoral Society*. New York: Charles Scribner's Sons, 1952.

Polanyi, Michael, *The Tacit Dimension*. Garden City, New York: Doubleday, 1967.

Riesman, David, *Constraint and Variety in American Education*. Lincoln, Nebraska: University of Nebraska Press, 1956.

Rudolph, Frederick, *The American College and University: A History*. New York: Alfred A. Knopf, 1962.

Schön, Donald, *The Reflective Practitioner: How Professionals Think in Action*. London: Basic Books, 1983.

Steiner, George, *Language and Silence: Essays on Language, Literature, and the Inhuman*. New York: Atheneum, 1967.

Thomas, Lewis, *Late Night Thoughts on Listening to Mahler's Ninth Symphony*. New York: The Viking Press, 1983.

Van Doren, Mark, *Liberal Education*. Boston: Beacon Press, 1959.

White, E. B., "One Man's Meat," *Harper's Magazine,* vol. 177 (October 1938).

BIBLIOGRAPHY

Bibliography

Books Written by Ernest L. Boyer

Boyer, Ernest L., *The Basic School: A Community for Learning*, The Carnegie Foundation for the Advancement of Teaching, 1995.

——, *College: The Undergraduate Experience in America* (New York: Harper & Row, 1987).

——, *High School: A Report on Secondary Education in America* (New York: Harper & Row, 1983).

——, *Ready to Learn: A Mandate for the Nation*, The Carnegie Foundation for the Advancement of Teaching, 1991.

——, *Scholarship Reconsidered: Priorities of the Professoriate*, The Carnegie Foundation for the Advancement of Teaching, 1990.

Boyer, Ernest L., Philip G. Altbach, and Mary Jean Whitelaw, *The Academic Profession: An International Perspective*, The Carnegie Foundation for the Advancement of Teaching, 1994.

Boyer, Ernest L. and Fred M. Hechinger, *Higher Learning in the Nation's Service,* The Carnegie Foundation for the Advancement of Teaching, 1981.

Boyer, Ernest L. and Arthur Levine, *A Quest for Common Learning: The Aims of General Education*, A Carnegie Foundation Essay, The Carnegie Foundation for the Advancement of Teaching, 1981.

Boyer, Ernest L. and Lee D. Mitgang, *Building Community: A New Future for Architecture Education and Practice*, The Carnegie Foundation for the Advancement of Teaching, 1996.

Other Books Published by The Carnegie Foundation, 1981–1997

Boyer, Paul, *Native American Colleges: Progress and Prospects*, 1997.

The Carnegie Foundation for the Advancement of Teaching, *Campus Life: In Search of Community*, with a foreword by Ernest L. Boyer, 1990.

——, *A Classification of Institutions of Higher Education*, 1987.

——, *A Classification of Institutions of Higher Education*, with a foreword by Ernest L. Boyer, 1994.

——, *Common Learning: A Carnegie Colloquium on General Education*, 1981.

——, *The Condition of Teaching: A State-by-State Analysis, 1988*, with a foreword by Ernest L. Boyer, 1988.

——, *The Condition of Teaching: A State-by-State Analysis, 1990*, with a foreword by Ernest L. Boyer, 1990.

——, *The Condition of the Professoriate: Attitudes and Trends, 1989*, with a foreword by Ernest L. Boyer, 1989.

——, *The Control of the Campus: A Report on the Governance of Higher Education*, with a foreword by Ernest L. Boyer, 1982.

——, *Ernest L. Boyer: Selected Speeches, 1979–1995*, 1997.

——, *An Imperiled Generation: Saving Urban Schools*, 1988.

——, *The International Academic Profession: Portraits of Fourteen Countries*, edited by Philip G. Altbach, with a foreword by Ernest L. Boyer, 1997.

——, *Report Card on School Reform: The Teachers Speak*, with an analysis by Ernest L. Boyer, 1988.

——, *School Choice*, with a foreword by Ernest L. Boyer, 1992.

———, *Tribal Colleges: Shaping the Future of Native America*, with a foreword by Ernest L. Boyer, 1989.

Ch'i, Hsi-sheng, *Toward a Global Community of Scholars: The Special Partnership Between The Carnegie Foundation for the Advancement of Teaching and China's National Center for Education Development Research, 1988–1997*, 1997.

Clark, Burton R., *The Academic Life: Small Worlds, Different Worlds*, with a foreword by Ernest L. Boyer, 1987,

Eurich, Nell P., *Corporate Classrooms: The Learning Business*, with a foreword by Ernest L. Boyer, 1985.

———, *The Learning Industry: Education for Adult Workers*, with a foreword by Ernest L. Boyer, 1990.

Feistritzer, C. Emily, *The Condition of Teaching: A State-by-State Analysis, 1985*, with a foreword by Ernest L. Boyer, 1985.

Harrison, Charles H., *Student Service: The New Carnegie Unit*, with a foreword by Ernest L. Boyer, 1987.

Maeroff, Gene I., *School and College: Partnerships in Education*, with a foreword by Ernest L. Boyer, 1983.

McLaughlin, Judith Block and David Riesman, *Choosing a College President: Opportunities and Constraints*, with a foreword by Ernest L. Boyer, 1990.

Newman, Frank, *Higher Education and the American Resurgence*, with an introduction by Ernest L. Boyer, 1985.

Pelikan, Jaroslav, *Scholarship and Its Survival: Questions on the Idea of Graduate Education*, with a foreword by Ernest L. Boyer, 1983.

Stearns, Kathryn, *School Reform: Lessons from England*, with a foreword by Ernest L. Boyer, 1996.

Vito Perrone and Associates, *Portraits of High Schools: A Supplement to High School: A Report on Secondary Education in America*, 1985.